CONFEDERATE
TREASURE
IN
DANVILLE

J. Frank Carroll

I would like to acknowledge the following individuals for permission to reprint or paraphrase the following material.

Chapter I
Credit To Tales (Tale 4, D-Concealed In The Bank of Danville) from The Danville Register (*March* 16, 1948 *article re: Demolition of The Old Robertson Building*) **by Danville Register, © 1948.**
Reprinted and/or paraphrased by permission of The Register Publishing Company. All rights reserved.

Chapter I
Credit To Tales (Tales 10 through 21) *No Jubilee: The Story of Confederate Wilkes* **by Robert Willingham, Jr., © 1976. Reprinted and/or paraphrased by permission of author, Robert Willingham, Jr., 405 S. Alexander Ave., Washington, Georgia 30673. All rights reserved.**

Chapter II B - The Company Clerk
and Chapter III B - The Secretary In Absentia:
George Alfred Trenholm and The Company That Went To War 1861-1865
by Ethel Trenholm Seabrook Nepveux, © 1973., 1994.
Reprinted and/or paraphrased by permission of author.
All rights reserved.
Mrs. Ethel S. Nepveux, 717 Parish Rd., Charleston, SC 29407.

Publisher:
URE Press
Suite 500
636B Piney Forest Road
Danville, VA 24540

Cover design by Vaden & Associates

TABLE OF CONTENTS

"Lay not up for yourselves treasures upon earth, where moth and rust doth corrupt, and where thieves break through and steal: But lay up for yourselves treasures in heaven, where neither moth nor rust doth corrupt, and where thieves do not break through nor steal: For where your treasure is, there will your heart be also."

Matthew 6 : 19-21

FOREWORD

The preacher loosened a starched shirt collar, lowered his open Bible to the podium, adjusted his spectacles and read this Scripture lesson forty-four years ago when I was merely a dozen years old, living in Reidsville, North Carolina.

A quarter of a century later I moved to Danville, Virginia. After transferring to this river city I heard tales about the Confederate gold missing since the end of the Civil War. These rumors nagged, intrigued and challenged me. This mysterious, gilded gossip about a fortune that has eluded discovery for 131 years inspired research into it for a period of eighteen years. It has led me to conclude that at least a portion of this Confederate treasure is indeed buried beneath the sunlit surface of Danville, Virginia.

My quest for the treasure began with a penny postcard from Rev. Bob Snead to Rev. Paul Roberts which arrived on Saturday, August 4, 1951 in Reidsville, North Carolina announcing a church revival.

REVIVAL . . .
RIVERVIEW BAPTIST CHURCH
DANVILLE, VIRGINIA
AUGUST 6-11, 1951
SPECIAL SINGING EVERY NIGHT
EVERYONE WELCOME

Mr. Hudson, rural mail carrier, delivered this card to the mailbox in front of the log-house parsonage situated beside the church.

Years earlier, stone masons had constructed Wayside Baptist Church from large square chunks of Piedmont granite. Pastor Roberts had founded this church and bullied from its pulpit, where he announced the scheduled revival and urged his members to support Brother Snead's church in Danville.

Although hampered by a stale, breezeless heat that encouraged laziness, on this Monday mother labored through chores so we could obey our pastor's heeding. Our parents, cajoled by the pastor into attendance, urged this duty upon my 10-year-old sibling, Phillip, and me. After an early supper, our family of four piled into our dark-green Willys Jeep station wagon to attend the night-time services. The forty-five minute trip to Danville took just enough time for two lads in the back seat to play a game of *Counting and Burying Cows.*

Dad found a parking place in the church's graveled lot. When we arrived the service had already begun. Steamy gospel music, the best I had ever heard, streamed from open church windows and blended with summer heat.

In the sanctuary Dad located, as near as possible to the front, a partially-empty pew for our family. Mother found a funeral-home fan in the hymnal rack and, waving it back and forth, helped cool herself and her sons.

Nearby, brown-haired and petite Geneva Gentry arranged sheet music, raised up from the seat and squirmed slightly to remove an irritating wrinkle from her dress [æ] Comfort and creativity often share equal billing on the piano bench. Pauline Snead, whose long hair was "done up" in a bun, waited patiently to sing an appropriate hymn *I'm A Child Of the King*, while Geneva, whose style was to be admired, played an introduction. Phillip, impressed, leaned over and whispered to his mother, "She can really tear up a piano." After lively hymn-singing, special music and a prayer, the speaker entered the pulpit.

The heavenly-treasure sermon, based on Matthew 6: 19-21, captivated attention. But for me, the partly factual introductory story was more intriguing:

"Did you know that Jefferson Davis and his Cabinet brought the remnants of the failed Confederate government to Danville, Virginia, April 3-11, 1865? It's true," he said, "that's how Danville became known as *The Last Capital Of The Confederacy.* On Davis' train were treasure chests containing a fortune in gold and silver, more money than you or I will ever see on this earth. And, believe it or not, no one has found this Confederate money. All kinds of tales have been told about the whereabouts of the Confederate gold but no one has ever come up with it. Some people even say it's buried underneath Danville. Could be; I don't know. But if you ever find it, come and tell me where it is, and I'll help to dig it up . . ."

The minister returned to serious matters, intoning that spiritual treasure is far more important than any gold you could find on earth.

That evening in August, 1951, I vowed to do three things: To begin a search to find heavenly treasure; to study piano playing; and to find the missing Confederate gold.

Vow number one was satisfied when I, as a young man, barely fourteen, made a profession of faith, later confirmed by baptism. While my personal journey in Christian faith has been fraught with slippery stones, treacherous curves and occasional side paths, I am more committed than ever to seek heavenly treasure.

My parents bought a heavy upright piano so old that its varnish had darkened, and this piano sat prominently in our living room. Dad paid for piano lessons, and I happily let my "fingers do the walking", vivace, through five John Thompson books.

Soon I was able to escape, by improvisation, the playing of hymnals and sheet music. Such freedom permitted experimentation and was used in evangelistic crusades in nearly every state and in seventeen European countries. My goal to "tear up a piano" was *fait accompli*.

That sermon also set me on a fortune-hunting expedition to find the hidden Confederate gold. My following the treasure trail has led me to investigate numerous tales that have littered the landscape with dead ends.

In this book you will learn how honor, integrity, honesty, secrecy, deceit, death, lies and tall tales have been unlikely allies in keeping the interment intact. In some bizarre way, all of these became friends of the deceased.

Fallacious footprints made by following erroneous stories have made the treasure trail difficult to follow. Some treasure tales have just enough truth in them so that false leads seem credible. Others are filled with so many mistakes that sensible questions will spotlight the error and keep you on track. A few are folly, plain and simple, and do not deserve a second glance.

Before making this treasure trek, one must listen to many stories. Although the treasure tales that have been told are legion, skimpy evidence must be ferreted out piece by piece. On this expedition, one must stop over and over again to check for veracity.

That sermon, nearly a half century ago, had fragmented information, fallacies and some false notions. Over the years, some erroneous treasure tales have been repeated so often, and with such conviction, that they unjustly merit credibility. These yarns do nothing more than tamper with the evidence.

The careful reader of this book will find **real** evidence, just as I have, that will lead to attaining my third goal, discovering CONFEDERATE TREASURE IN DANVILLE.

Clues, good and bad, have existed for over a century. Books, letters, manuscripts, maps, newspapers, private letters, records, research papers and even weather reports have made significant contributions to help unravel the story of the missing Confederate treasure.

Some people deserve special recognition for their contributions.

I am grateful to all those whose speculations, claims, and stories inspired me to dig deeper for more truth about the whereabouts of the Confederate treasure.

My Sincere Thanks Go Out To . . .

Mary Cahill, Phillip G. Carroll, Claude Chambers, Tom Dareneau, Kathy Davis, Dr. Sam Fletcher, Clara Fountain, Petie Bogan-Garrett, Angela Gatewood, Gary Grant, Bill Grier, Marillyn Halstead, Kay Harbison, Paul Kelley, William Luebke, Ethel Trenholm Seabrook Nepveux, Wilbert Long, Jr., Dr. Linda McCurdy, Lawrence McFall, Dr. Joyce Nestor, Reference Librarians of the Dahlonega Public Library, Reference Librarians of The Danville Public Library, Reference Librarians of the Virginia State Library, Danny Ricketts, Guy Swanson, George E. Turner, and Minor Weisiger.

And especially to . . .

Dr. James I. Robertson, Jr., without whose encouragement this story would have continued to be buried beneath the piedmont soil of Danville, Virginia, The Last Capital of the Confederacy.

But Most Of All To . . .

Dottie van Haaften, whose hands and eyes substituted for mine and inspired me to persevere to the end.

Two shovels, mental and physical, are necessary in order to dig for buried treasure. This book deals entirely with the mental aspect. Without that, the physical shovel isn't worth a visit to your local hardware store. Dogged research followed by extensive analyses, common sense and circumstances are, of course, necessary ingredients.

Many years have passed since I was at the National Archives and the Library of Congress learning all I could about the Confederate treasure.

Those hours in dusty books whetted my appetite for many more hours of research. Genealogy, geography, meteorology, psychology and myriad other disciplines were employed to complete the jigsaw puzzle. As each new piece of the puzzle was discovered, it confirmed itself and lent credence to the next one, logically continuing the process until a clear picture emerged. Finally, I was convinced about the whereabouts of a portion of the treasure, as I'm certain you will be, too.

A warning though. A casual glance through this book, choosing highlighted portions, will not work! You must read the entire book to be convinced.

Civil War author/historian, Burke Davis, aptly named the nearly two months at the end of the four-year conflict *The Long Surrender*. It is ironic that while the Confederacy was in its dying throes, the Confederate treasure was only beginning to live. Although most of the bounty from that treasure was distributed in 1865, heretofore uncovered facts lend credibility to that continued life.

Confederate Treasure in Danville reawakens interest in an almost forgotten fortune that has secretly slumbered in undisturbed earth for 131 years. Now, the silvery voice of that sleepy treasure calls out from its resting place and draws attention to a city on the Dan River.

CREDIT TO TALES

The Confederate treasure had barely departed Richmond when rumors, speculation, secrecy and lies formed layers of protection around the contents and concealed the whereabouts of the cache from a curious public. "Rumors had circulated about the treasure and with each retelling the size grew."

The legends surrounding the wagons of the Confederate treasure are legion, but somewhere amid the extraordinary stories emerge a sizable amount of fiction and a fractional amount of truth.

Written treasure tales have appeared in newspapers, letters, articles, official records and books. Spoken ones have been in whispered gossip, family reminiscences, and rumors, as well as in lectures. Films also have made contributions to the legend of the lost loot.

It would be impossible to reiterate all of the tales that have been told about the Confederate treasure. One would have to listen to generations of gossip, a century of cocktail party chatter, scads of serious discussions and intellectual theories; read thousands of newspaper accounts, private letters, books and view multitudes of movies.

Some selected stories bear repeating. They are factual, fictional, foolish, fantastic and fun. Perhaps the best kept secrets about the Confederate treasure survived for well over a century on the back of tall tales.

1. Major General Stoneman

Six-foot-four-inch Major General George Stoneman of the Federal forces had "orders to destroy." This giant warrior fulfilled his command by tearing up three hundred miles of railroad tracks, terrorizing rebel citizens and chasing the fleeing Confederate government. Obsessed with this task, he bragged about his intentions to capture the Confederate treasure and pursued it with a vengeance.

Captain Parker's book *Recollections of a Naval Officer* described it this way, "It was supposed he [Stoneman] would obtain information there [Salisbury, North Carolina] concerning the treasure, and that he would soon make his appearance in Charlotte where there were no troops to oppose him." Why this never occurred no one knows. Parker continued, "We supposed General Stoneman to be in pursuit with his cavalry . . . We thought at the time he would get news of the treasure at Charlotte and follow us."

Due to blind determination, Stoneman believed rumors that the treasure could be worth as much as $13,000,000; was foolish enough to file official reports based on these rumors and even had the audacity to leak these fallacious reports to newspapers. Citizens from the North and the South, who were fooled by his ardor, believed his tales and perpetuated his speculations.

Robert M. Willingham, Jr's book, *No Jubilee: The Story of Confederate Wilkes* confirmed these rambling stories of incredible riches. It goes something like this: "$13,000,000. Yes, thirteen million dollars! That was the amount supposed by Union General Stoneman to be carried by the treasure train which was making its way haltingly from Richmond to the south by rail and wagon." The fantastic amount reported by General Stoneman was not anywhere close to the truth.

Hearing reports of Stoneman's rumors, the last acting treasurer of the Confederate States of America, M. H. Clark, attempted to clarify these false allegations. "Owing to the great weight of silver which we carried, it was reported, and generally believed, that we had some $2,000,000 to $10,000,000". What folly! The combined treasures, Confederate treasure and Virginia bank funds, could not have amounted to more than $1,000,000 in specie. Clark continued, "In reality, such a vast horde of gold and silver was ridiculous. Remember, the Confederacy was, for the most part, even unable to pay its soldiers and purchase supplies during the last year of the war." Yet even with these limitations Clark admitted, "there was still specie and a sizable amount, although no one knows exactly how much."

The only definitive statement available regarding the value of the Confederate treasure alone, when it departed Richmond April 3, 1865, was provided by Walter Philbrook, Chief Teller of the Treasury Department. Philbrook arrived at this figure because Mann S. Quarles, a treasury clerk, "had the good sense to total the contents of each container holding specie, label each with the Seal of the Confederate States of America," record those amounts on rough paper and present these totals to him. Having been authorized by the Secretary of the Treasury to be in charge of the treasure as it left Richmond, Philbrook reported that the Confederate treasure contained between $500,000 and $600,000 in specie.

2. James Jones

Another tale about the treasure that many people believed and was publicized heavily is merely a case of pure fiction. James Jones, Davis' trusted mulatto servant, with an inordinate thirst for notoriety, gave to the press a carefully elaborated narrative which declared that President Davis had entrusted the Great Seal to his care, and that he had sunk it in the James River near Richmond. He claimed that he had been entrusted also with a treasure amounting to $13,000,000, which he had hauled round on a freight-car "from one point to another in the South until Captain Parker . . . relieved me of it at a point near Washington, Georgia."

Both statements were entirely false; but the story appealed to the public's love of adventure, and for many years it continued to be repeated as history. As late as June 4, 1907, the New York daily *Tribune* printed three columns of Jones' "Memories" which had still lost nothing of their popular appeal.

3. Somewhere Between Richmond and Danville

The exodus of the treasure train from Richmond began midnight April 3, 1865. Traveling at a speed of 9-10 miles per hour, those on board were fearful of being captured if the train had stopped for any reason. Also, had the treasure been buried en route, the treasury clerks would have violated the direct written orders to Walter Philbrook to bring the entire treasure, intact, to Danville. Several well-documented accounts confirmed that Chief Teller Philbrook did not violate those orders.

4. Danville, Virginia

A. Buried Under Stratford College Main Building

This story has been repeated over drinks for many years. Since Stratford College main building was not constructed until 1883, the Confederate treasure could not have been buried there.

A less well-authenticated story is that some of the overflow of boxes containing specie were stored in the attic of the building now known as Stratford College.

There are no documents to support this theory, only gossip, fueled by an article published in the *Bee*, Danville's afternoon edition, March 16, 1948. Besides, common sense would deny the possibility of its ever having been kept there because students and faculty would have noticed the cache and could have possibly returned later to claim the specie.

B. Buried Underneath Sutherlin Mansion Front Stairs

Discussions of this location come to the fore as soon as missing Confederate treasure is mentioned. The front stairs of

Sutherlin Mansion, Circa 1870 (Courtesy of Museum of Fine Arts & History)

Major Sutherlin's house had already been constructed when the treasure arrived in Danville in 1865.

1. Common sense denies the front stairs theory for the following reasons:

A sentry was posted at the front gate of the Sutherlin Mansion. No one was permitted to enter or leave the Sutherlin Mansion without announcing their intentions. Those same front stairs were equally as active - day or night.

2. Four wagon loads of treasure would have to have entered the front gate which was less than four feet wide posing a problem of dimension. Too many people would have to have been consulted to resolve the quandary of the logistics. These same people would have returned later to unearth the cache.

3. The front stairs (while in constant use) would have had to be removed. A chasm approximately four feet wide, twenty feet long and six feet deep would have to have been dug creating a huge amount of curiosity which surely would have been reported.

C. Buried Anywhere on Sutherlin Mansion Property

Speculators tenaciously refuse to give up on the Sutherlin Mansion property as the burial site. When the front stairs theory is repudiated, they look for alternative sites on the Sutherlin grounds as a possibility.

The entire four-acre Sutherlin property was a flurry of activity in 1865 and therefore subject to continuous scrutiny by the Sutherlin family, the house staff and Confederate officials æ day and night.

Two tent encampments occupied a large portion of the grounds. Captain Given Campbell's scouts and couriers were located there, as well as the three men who made up the President's Guard. Their purpose for being there was to watch over the President. Since so many keen observers were there, the treasure could never have been buried anywhere on the Sutherlin Mansion property.

D. Concealed in The Bank of Danville

One story with a Danville origin was introduced by a

Bank of Danville *(Courtesy of Danville Historical Society)*

former professor at Randolph Macon Woman's College in Danville (now closed). In March 1948, when interviewed by a reporter for a newspaper article, Professor Meade discussed the old Robertson building which was about to be demolished:

"Before many weeks, the wreckers will be again in charge of a Main Street building æ the old 'Robertson Building ' æ at the crest of Main Street hill." The old Robertson Building opposite the Elks Home was about to be pulled down to make room for a third liquor store in town.

Dr. Meade and other local historians had advanced an idea that, "the building was thought to rate a metal marker as the last known Treasury of the Confederacy," but the movement never got very far. It was in this building that boxes of specie and bullion, together with other important papers "were housed when Jefferson Davis left Richmond for the week's interregnum in Danville."

Professor Robert Douthat Meade of Randolph Macon Woman's College faculty wrote a biography of Judah P. Benjamin, "who came to Danville with Davis and who occupied a room on Wilson Street." Meade was quite sure that the Robertson building was used for the purpose cited.

"He found allusions to it while engaged in intensive research on the Benjamin book, later wrote an article about Danville's historical, but unrecognized buildings."

Continuing the interview, Dr. Meade reported, "When the bullion had been stowed, a guard was posted over the building." Dr. Meade understood that when Davis and his entourage found that it was time to move farther south (Greensboro) the cases of cash and notes were entrained (April 6, 1865).

The newspaper article went on to state that the building about to be wrecked was virtually the same building used by President Davis to store the Confederate treasure. Adding to the mystery and intrigue about this treasure, the reporter wrote, "When its timbers are bared there may be some hidden treasure-trove in the rafters, between the walls, or under the floor."

The professor did his homework. Many written records establish that he was telling the truth, as much as he knew it.

However, when the building was demolished, no Confederate treasure was found.

E. Buried in Grove Street Cemetery

Some wide-eyed gold diggers have surmised that the treasure must be buried in Grove Street Cemetery. The three reasons cited most often are:

The cemetery was receiving interments in 1865.

It was in close proximity to the Sutherlin Mansion.

Who would be foolish enough to exhume graves?

It is possible that the treasure could be buried here. Proponents of this theory are correct that Grove Street Cemetery was actively receiving interments in 1865. However, its close proximity to the Sutherlin Mansion may be the best reason to remove it from consideration as a likely burial site simply because of the large number of people who would have probably observed gravediggers at work when there was no corpse.

F. Buried in Green Hill Cemetery

Rumors are also rampant regarding Green Hill Cemetery as a likely place for the burial of the Confederate treasure. Many good reasons have been proffered. Consider these:

It had been receiving interments since 1863.

It was located five minutes from the Confederate States Offices on Wilson Street.

Who would chance desecrating a cemetery in order to dig for buried treasure?

It is possible that the treasure could be buried here. However, there is one glaring drawback. The prison hospital was located less than 1,000 yards away. The possiblity looms that one of the infirmed may have been watching.

G. Major Edward Sixtus Hutter of the Danville Arsenal

Some people thought that Judah Benjamin retrieved a portion of the gold from the treasure train parked near Linn Street and freely shared it with selected Danvillians. This simply was not true but was based in large part on the following written account, "While conversing with Major Edward S. Hutter, commander of the Danville arsenal, Benjamin asked him if he had been paid recently and, finding that he had not, gave him $600." This was the amount due him, in gold belonging to the government. Benjamin is supposed to have said, "The Confederate soldiers had better have the gold than the Yankees."

Major Edward Sixtus Hutter
(Courtesy of Evaline J. Wood)

H. Danville Forgotten

Several authors have written, "When the Confederate government abandoned Richmond as its capital, all its archives and treasures were sent under strong military escort to Charlotte, N. C." The banks of Richmond sent away their funds under protection of the same guard.

These tales are confusing in that they incorrectly imply that President Davis and his Cabinet accompanied the treasure all the way to Charlotte, North Carolina. President Davis and his cabinet were seldom in the presence of the treasure.

The Presidential train left Richmond one hour ahead of the treasure train. On April 6, the treasure train departed Danville for Greensboro while President Davis and his cabinet remained in Danville for five more days. The treasure train continued to Charlotte on April 7, 1865 while the Confederate officials were still in Danville.

For some unexplained reason, many authors completely ignore the fact that the Confederacy established its capital in Danville, Virginia from April 3-10, 1865. Because these authors mentioned other towns and cities along the evacuation route, and failed to mention the little town on the southside of Virginia, Danville has been often forgotten.

I. Dr. G. W. Dame Story

"Didn't George W. Dame have something to do with hiding the Confederate gold?" This question and many similar ones imply that the Episcopal rector could have hidden a substantial portion of the Confederate Treasure.

These speculations have been generated by the following written document that really occurred after President Davis and his cabinet had fled farther south. "During the month of the stay of the Federal soldiers in Danville, officers and men were daily in the rector's study." No doubt every day at sunset the rector rejoiced afresh that no soldier had thought to notice the half-burned wood and ashes which filled the open fireplace. Hidden underneath the ashes in a tin box was all the actual capital ($2,000 in gold) of the Danville Bank, which the bank directors had requested Dr. Dame to hold and hide for them. For, as they said, "This is liable to seizure by the Federal soldiers, and you, because of your well-known activity in aid of the prisoners, may be able to protect it for us, and keep it safe."

J. Levi Holbrook Questions

Several facts and a plethora of speculation surround this enigmatic man, who was living in the Sutherlin Mansion during the time Jefferson Davis and his Cabinet were there.

Levi Holbrook was a school teacher who attained great wealth while living in Danville. At one time, more than sixty percent of all the specie in the Bank of Danville belonged to him. His money continued to increase during the war while everyone else suffered losses. Whispers, rumors and gossip about this strange man led to one query after another.

"Why was he so private?"
"How was it possible for one to derive such an
enormous sum of money from teaching?"
"What was the source of his fortune?"
"Could he have overheard where the treasure
was hidden and secretly dug it up after the war?"
"If he were so rich, why did he live so miserly?"
"Did he have something to hide?"

These questions are valid. While there are few substantive documents to answer these inquiries, their absence nurtures more questions. Since he was an extremely intelligent man, could he have created a clever cover-up to eliminate self-incriminating records about the source of his wealth?

5. *Gone With The Wind* Theory

It is generally thought the model for Margaret Mitchell's character Rhett Butler in *Gone With The Wind*, was the last Secretary of the Treasury for the C.S.A., George A. Trenholm.

Ethel Trenholm Seabrook Nepvuex, in her book, *George Alfred Trenholm and The Company That Went To War* describes her great-grandfather not only as a smart businessman, "he was also a swashbuckler who took huge risks resulting in great success or equally great losses. He had money, and the courage to make more of it."

Someone wrote that George A. Trenholm "made off with and buried the gold of the Confederate Treasury." The only **proof** presented for this statement was a remark made by the character Aunt Pittypat in *Gone With The Wind* when she said Rhett Butler had told her he had stolen the gold.

In a published letter, Ethel refuted this allegation, "That is hearsay, spoken by a fictitious individual in a fictitious book. No proof has ever been suggested that George Trenholm buried this treasure."

6. Judah P. Benjamin Tales

Because Judah P. Benjamin, the Secretary of State, successfully eluded capture by the Federal troops and made his getaway to England, some historians have speculated that he was also able to take the Confederate gold with him. This would seem to be a logical conclusion. Both were not only missing, but missing at the same time.

A large number of historical documents relate that Benjamin requested and received $1,500 in gold (for secret service work) from the Confederate States Treasury before leaving Richmond. As if to provide funds in case of removal of the capital, treasury warrants were issued to various Confederate officials. "One warrant, dated 1 April 1865, which is still in existence, was issued to Benjamin on the 'Secret Service' account. It was for $1,500 in gold, and receipt for payment was signed by C. W. Volkman, a clerk in the State Department."

Was Benjamin also preparing in case it would be necessary for him to escape from the South? Issuance of the treasury warrant indicated that he may have been doing so, as did the fact that by [date unknown] March his chief clerk, William J. Bromwell, had already been sent southward with a number of boxes and trunks of valuable papers. On April 5, Bromwell wrote Benjamin from Lexington, North Carolina, that they had all been stored in Charlotte, North Carolina: six boxes of papers belonging to the State Department which had been marked 'W.J.B.' 'to attract as little attention as possible'; two trunks marked 'J.P.B.,' one 'G.D.,' one 'D. F. Kenner,' and one 'St. Martin.'

This same data reports that after leaving the Presidential party he made a unilateral escape to Florida. Near the village of Manatee, he stayed at the home of Captain Frederick Tresca. When Benjamin revealed that he was carrying $1,500 in gold, Mrs. Tresca offered to help him conceal the money by sewing it into the back of his waistcoat.

It would have been both awkward and uncomfortable for Judah Benjamin to lug around the tremendous weight and bulk associated with such a large sum of Confederate gold. The seventy-five $20 gold pieces on his person weighed five pounds. He must have experienced how unwieldy the specie was because one document stated that he sent $300 of this total to relatives. Even the sixty $20 gold pieces remaining were a bulky and heavy companion.

7. Three Tales Involving "False Bottom Of A Carriage"

Eli Evans, in *Judah P. Benjamin*, says that the last of the treasury money was sent to Charleston in the false bottom of a carriage to be smuggled to England for future guerrilla action from the West.

If the last of the treasure money were $86,000, that would not have been enough to finance any significant military threat. Keep in mind that these 4,300 coins would have weighed approximately 286 pounds.

In *Flight Into Oblivion*, A. J. Hanna gives a long description of the care and disposition of the Confederate assets on pages 90-116. On page 91, he writes that W. H. Clark "paid to James A. Semple, a bonded officer of the Navy, who, with an assistant, agreed to take it, concealed under the false bottom of a carriage, to Charleston or Savannah and then ship to a Confederate agent in Bermuda, Nassau, or Liverpool, or some other foreign port for the account of the Confederate government about $86,000."

Again, the amount suggested would have financed little more than a few skirmishes and would not have been adequate to reverse the eventual outcome of the fall of the Confederate government.

A third story presented not only confusion about the contents, but also about the chronology. "It was concealed in the false bottom of a carriage and sent to Charleston or Savannah for shipment to a Confederate agent overseas."

Stories like this one bewildered those who attempted to trace the eventual disposition of the Confederate treasure.

8. Virginia Bank Funds and Confederate Treasure Mix-Up

Two separate treasures, the **Virginia bank funds** and the Confederate treasure, departed Richmond on the same midnight train April 3, 1865.

The **Virginia bank funds** were supervised by Judge W. W. Crump, who was assisted by junior clerks from six banks. The bank funds were placed in the second forty-four-foot-long freight car, earmarked with the stamp of each bank. These boxes were not opened during the journey south.

By contrast, the Confederate treasure was placed under the care of Walter Philbrook, Chief Teller of the Confederate Treasury. It was packed in boxes, bags, chests and kegs which were labeled with the seal of the Confederacy and located in the first freight car. Clerks from the Confederate Treasury judicially insured the integrity of their charge on its way south, never permitting the conjoining of monies.

Although the private funds and public monies **were never mixed**, some stories failed to keep them separate, resulting in muddled messages about both funds.

Puzzlement resulted from the fact that William Parker and the sixty midshipmen gave protection to the Confederate treasure and the **Virginia bank funds**. Since both treasures left Richmond under the same strong military escort, it was assumed by those who didn't know the facts, that the two treasures were one and the same.

9. *White Columns In Georgia* **Theory**

In her book *White Columns in Georgia*, Medora Field Perkerson wrote a chapter entitled, "Lost Gold of the Confederacy," in which she outlines the movements of the treasure under the Confederate Navy Captain William Harwar Parker, assisted by Confederate midshipmen. Mrs. Perkerson leaves some of the money unexplained, with legend saying that it was buried in Washington, Georgia.

Like so many before her, Mrs. Perkerson fell into the trap of combining **Virginia bank funds** with Confederate treasure, thereby making a difficult trail even more perplexing to follow.

10. **Vaughan's Brigade Tale**

The most completely presented tale found in Robert Willingham, Jr.'s book *No Jubilee: The Story of Confederate Wilkes* should be repeated as written.

"Lewis Shepherd of Tennessee, a member of Vaughan's Brigade, and, although not acknowledged, perhaps a member of the raiding party, recalled vividly the events of that May 24th;"

Evidently some of the officers and men of Vaughan's Brigade discovered that a train of specie was being carried north under Federal escort. They jumped to the conclusion that it was the property of the Confederate government which the Federals had captured. They concluded that their four years of hard service for the Confederacy entitled them to a share of this gold and silver, provided they could succeed in securing it from the Federal guard. They justified their actions because in their estimation the war was not yet over, and anything is fair in war. They organized an expedition to capture this money and followed the train intent upon attack. They charged the train, captured and disarmed the guard. The soldiers knocked the heads from the kegs and removed the lids from the coin boxes. They filled their forage sacks with gold eagles and double eagles.

Amounts taken ranged from a high of $60,000 to a low of $4,000 depending upon the carrying capacity of their sacks and saddlebags.

One man filled his sack out of the first keg he came to, which proved to be a keg of silver. "He was happy when he lugged off his bag of silver dollars; but when he met his companions later in the rendezvous, where they stopped to count the money, he had only about $4,000 while his companions had several times that sum in gold." When they refused to share their wealth, he decided to turn informer. With the information furnished by him, several of the gold bugs were apprehended and forced to give up their booty. But a number of them kept going until they got safely away.

Lewis Shepherd goes on with his story, "Two men went with more than $120,000 to Kansas City, Missouri," becoming wealthy business men. Two others became California business men with something their $100,000. A rich Texas planter began his business with some of the silver while another Texan started a successful cattle business. **The Richmond banks spent large sums in vain efforts to recover their money.**

When news of this raid had been received in Washington, General Edward Porter Alexander quickly organized a company and **rode to the aid of the bank officials.** Judge William Reese accompanied them with warrants hoping there could be a speedy apprehension. Alexander's party captured several of them but Judge Reese refused to issue warrants. He was afraid that since his appointment as judge had been under Confederate law, the Federals might accuse him of usurping his authority.

Nevertheless, Alexander and his men were able to recover almost $120,000 of the funds. Despite Alexander's explanation that the stolen property was private, not Confederate, treasure, there were several episodes of drawn pistols, but no actual violence. Four men arrested by Alexander had almost $80,000 with them. The money was retrieved but the citizens of Danburg prevented Alexander's men from taking the prisoners back to Washington.

Willingham wrote that, "Many tales have evolved from this episode in Confederate history, the Federal occupation force being particularly attuned to any ripe legend." For weeks they questioned and intimidated local citizens. In their panic, many of them buried even their private silver and what little money they might have had.

Remember, this tale appeared more chaotic because **Virginia bank funds** were incorrectly identified as Confederate treasure.

11. One Thousand Dollars

A humorous story in Willingham's book went something like this, "One gentleman near Danburg who had acquired $1,000 in specie, was too late in his attempt to hide his treasure. Hearing Federal horsemen approaching and unable to bury the money, he tossed the sack over his hedge to put it out of sight and in the process smashed the passing Federal officer on the head with his sack of specie."

This story was also referring to **Virginia bank funds** and not the Confederate treasure. Since this book is about the missing Confederate treasure, this particular tale has no bearing on the concealment and ultimate location of the Confederate cache.

12. Chennault Family Tale

Willingham's book narrated another often-repeated tale. "As darkness fell, the officers of the wagon train approached Reverend Dionysius Chennault and asked permission to camp on his property." The Reverened agreed and gave them an enclosed horse lot with a double gate in which to park their five wagons. Raiders struck quickly, shouting, cursing, shooting and ransacking the treasure train. Raiding horsemen loaded themselves down with gold and silver and spilled some along the way. The next morning, the **bank officials** were able to recover $40,000 which had been dropped by the attackers during the hasty night raid.

General Wilde commanded the garrison. His methods were dispicable. Angelina, a servant of the Chennault family came to him with great stories of gold and jewelry held by her former masters and promised to assist Wilde in his search.

When General Wilde and his troops rode up to Reverend Chennault's home, only the barking of a dog gave notice of their arrival. The dog, named *Jeff Davis* by the Chennault chil-

Rev. Dionysius Chennault House (Mercer Harris Photography)

dren, barked continually until Federal soldiers "shot him and then punctured him with bayonets while laughing, 'Kill Jeff Davis! Kill Jeff Davis!'" When Reverend Chennault's small cache of gold was found, watches were taken from the women. "John N. Chennault, his son Frank, and Reverend Chennault were arrested and taken into the adjacent woods." They were tortured to reveal where the stolen gold was hidden! Three times Reverend Chennault, who weighed over three hundred pounds, was lifted up by his thumbs until his feet left the ground. John and Frank Chennault endured similiar tortures, begging to be shot instead of having to abide such pain. Because the interrogation lasted all day and into the night, John Chennault finally fainted and the Federals thought him dead. Angelina's son, Tom, was also tortured repeatedly, but he professed to knowing nothing of the fortune in gold.

Meantime, other Federal soldiers terrorized the Chennault women and children. Family servants slipped the youngest children out of the house. Six-month-old John was taken to the nurse Mandy's cabin. Another Chennault child escaped on the back of maid Mary, who traveled over rough terrain and even waded a creek in order to reach Captain James Willis who was three miles away. The rest of the Channault children stayed at James Brooksdale's.

Angelina turned out to be more like the Devil than an angel. Mrs. Dionysius Chennault, Mrs. John N. Chennault, and her seventeen-year-old daughter, Mary Ann, were forced to strip in a locked room, and subjected to search and unspeakable indignities by Angelina. Afterwards, they joined the Chennault men and were taken to Washington, Georgia. The men were jailed while the women were locked in the jury room. Two attorneys, Samuel Barnett and Judge Andrews, were hired and they managed to secure the Chennault's release. As soon as they were freed, the money and jewelry which had been taken from them was returned. But they never could forget the horrors of their ordeal.

This appalling account referred to **Virginia bank funds** again and had absolutely nothing to do with the Confederate treasure. Failure to clarify this point has led many Confederate treasure hunters astray.

Matthews House (*Mercer Harris Photography*)

13. Bob, John and Joe Matthews

Who could forget the story of the Matthews boys as related in Willingham's book? It told about three young boys, Bob, John and Joe Matthews, who were neighbors of the Chennaults. One the morning after the raid while looking for cows, the boys noticed that horsemen had ridden through their property. Tracking the hooves of the horses, they discovered several thousand dollars hidden in a hollow tree stump. After revealing to their father, Fenton Matthews, what they had found, the money was turned over to General Alexander. Later, returning to the tree stump, even more money was discovered.

All of the money found was gold from the **Virginia bank funds.** This is another example of how easy it is to read about **Virginia bank funds** and not differentiate between them and the Confederate treasure. When these two treasures are kept separate, as they should be, the confusion is removed.

14. Specie Found In A Bureau Story

According to Sutton family reminiscences, almost $75,000 was found in a bureau at the hotel run by Mrs. John H. Walton at Danburg, Georgia.

This story may be a fabrication and not worthy for consideration. But even if it were true, **Virginia bank funds** are discussed in this story while most people are improperly thinking about the Confederate treasure.

15. Hull Evans Story

Another fictitious story is spawned in Willingham's book. In 1877, twelve years after the government fled from Richmond, an Athens, Georgia, newspaper account reported a story about Hull Evans, Washington's black barber who had moved to Wilkes County, Georgia from South Carolina near war's end. Evans, asked a customer what was the value of a bar of gold. The question immediately made Evans a local celebrity because many thought he knew the location of the gold. Revelling in his celebrity status, he intimated that he had several gold bars to sell. Locals believed his story, became frustrated, threatened and forced him to reveal the location of the gold. After he was released his, captors headed for the spot where they dug for hours, but found nothing.

In this case, the missing gold referred to bullion and not specie. The **Virginia bank funds** contained only specie. However, since all the gold bullion known to be in the Confederate treasure had already been dispensed, this story is relegated to a simple case of fabrication.

16. Booker Hill Story

Money-hungry hoodlums descended on another character as reported in *No Jubilee: The Story of Confederate Wilkes*. Three men attempted to kidnap Booker Hill, another black man, who was sitting in front of the Central Hotel of Augusta. Although the attempted abduction was unsuccessful, it was obvious why he was suspected. They thought he knew where the gold was hidden since he had been visiting Hull Evans in Washington. Nothing could have been more ridiculous. But the story kept being told. Years later in the 1880's, a pond near Delhi was drained in the belief that the gold rested on its bottom.

This story, while referring to the Confederate treasure, has no validity because it got caught up in the excitement of unfounded gossip.

Mrs. Royland Beasley House (Mercer Harris Photography)

17. Mrs. Royland Beasley Story

C.S. Navy midshipmen who guarded the Confederate treasure found residence at the home of Mrs. Royland Beasley, who was affectionally known as *Miss Kittie*. As the story goes, they brought their belongings as well as some heavy boxes. Supposedly, she was intrigued by their mysterious behavior. Around May 1, 1865, before leaving at night they gave her between $800 and $1000 in gold. They then told her that they had buried a large amount of gold under the ivy and periwinkle in her garden. After the middies had gone, Mrs. Beasley bought a store house and lot on the public square. Towards the end of 1865, two middies returned and told her some of the gold was accidently left buried. Again, they were permitted to dig in her garden but the ivy was gone and no gold was ever found.

This story is entirely false in that it states that the midshipmen had jurisdiction over part of the treasure. W. H. Parker's control over the midshipmen was so complete that he was able to order them to walk behind the treasure wagons until the soles of their shoes were worn through. Captain Parker, who maintained strict supervision over the midshipmen, did not have access to either of the treasures. He clearly emphasized that he never saw any of the coins.

Captain Parker did not believe it was in his purview to have intimate knowledge of the contents of the treasure wagons. If this were true, no one should believe that any of the midshipmen would have known either. He wrote about his knowledge of the contents of the Confederate treasure, "It was not my business to inquire."

18. Davis Doled Out Specie

Several authors have written that President Davis made efforts to prevent the capture of himself and the Confederate treasure. Some even wrote that he personally divided the treasure among the soldiers so that each received $26.50.

These stories, as written, falsely imply that President Jefferson Davis was personally concerned with and had control over both the **Virginia bank funds** and the Confederate treasure. Confusion results when **Virginia bank funds** and Confederate treasure are incorrectly reported as one. President Davis had nothing to do with the **Virginia bank funds** and pointedly avoided having anything to do with the Confederate treasure as well.

The truth is that the **officers of the banks** asked the Federal commanders to **return their specie to Richmond**. They were granted a permit and soldiers to guard it on its return trip.

This story is questionable in it's entirety because no significance is placed on the difference between the **Virginia bank funds** and the Confederate treasure.

19. The Last Confederate Payroll

The story of *The Last Confederate Payroll* has been forever believed as one of the most important documents to furnish corroboration for the final disposition of the Confederate treasure. It can be found in the *Confederate Military History, Volume II*. In that article is a biographical sketch of Major Joseph M. Broun. Major Broun recounted his opinion of what happened to the

Confederate treasure in this historical document.

The major who was there when it happened, got it confused because he failed to separate **Virginia bank funds** from the Confederate treasure.

This letter dated February 18, 1914 from Mr. W. E. R. Byrne confirms the confusion:

Judge Lewis Shepherd, Chattanooga, Tenn.—Dear Sir: Having seen in the Literary Digest of the 7th of February, 1914, your account of the disappearance of the Confederate treasure, my attention was called to a statement relative to the subject made by Maj. Joseph M. Broun, deceased. Major Broun died in this city on the 9th of December, 1908, and after his death there was found among his papers the statement in his own handwriting, a copy of which I take the liberty of inclosing.

Thinking it likely that these documents might throw, some additional light upon the subject and that they would be of interest to you, it occurred to me to send them for such use as you may see fit to make.

Yours very respectfully,   W. E. R. Byrne.

Major Broun's papers said that from April to May, 1865 he was a bonded quartermaster and estimated the value of the treasure to be $150,000. He further reported that this gold had been brought from Richmond, Va. guarded by midshipmen. "Because the enemy surrounded our troops, they had become demoralized about the gold." He said they predicted that the quartermaster or the Yankees would take the treasure if they didn't. Major Broun was afraid because there was no discipline. But General Breckinridge, dressed in an old Kentucky hunting jacket, appeared before the unruly soldiers. "Breckenridge told them they were Southern gentlemen and Confederate soldiers. They must not become highway robbers." He appealed to their honor, realizing that they not only knew how to die bravely; they also must live honorably. Breckenridge promised them an orderly distribution of enough of the gold to help each one on his way. Calmed and controlled, the soldiers became quiet and content.

Major Broun's tale bordered on being foolish.

He said that General Bragg, some of his staff, and himself went to the gold train where under General Bragg's directions they took about a quart of gold coin and tied it up in their handkerchiefs. With this treasure uncounted, they went to the town of Washington where he opened a pay office under the direction of General Bragg. He then said that each soldier received a twenty-dollar gold piece and gave him a receipt. "When the soldiers ceased coming," he said "there remained on the table two twenties and one ten." At this point Major Broun diversed into a flight of fantasy. He said that General Bragg turned and said to him, "Captain, you estimate closely. Receipt to yourself for what is left and close the account." Whereupon he pocketed the fifty dollars and signed the pay roll. At this point he couldn't resist romantizing the story even more, "Immediately after this payment we all disbanded, each man going his way. This was the last act of the Confederate government, so far as I know."

What follows in his account reveals how General Bragg and his men started the receipt list and gave it to him. Supposedly he gave the payroll list as a souvenir to Mrs. Pope, the wife of his intimate friend Willliam A. Pope, with whom he had been a schoolmate at Frank Minor's Ridgeway Academy.

He said that the residue of the gold was deposited in a bank vault at Washington, Ga. **Shortly after the surrender some bankers of Richmond, claiming this gold as their private property and denying that it ever had been Confederate property,** transported it back to Richmond, Va., overland in wagons before the railroads had been restored to operation. This gold train en route was partly robbed a time or two. Finally the United States government took charge of the gold which Broun estimated to be a hundred thousand dollars, and deposited it in the treasury at Washington.

Notice again the chaotic situation created because he failed to differentiate between Confederate treasure and **Virginia bank funds**. Also, Major Broun suffered from a bad case of self-aggrandizement.

It is impossible to understand the final disposition of the Confederate treasure based upon perplexing information like this.

20. Morris Sheppard Story

A story was published in the Chattanooga *Times* on Sunday, March 15, 1914. In this article, Judge Lewis Shepherd was seeking information about the fortune of gold coin and bullion presumably captured by Federals on their flight south.

Evidently, Judge Shepherd wrote to his relative, Morris Sheppard [note spelling], Senator from Texas, seeking further information about the treasure. Senator Sheppard answered with a letter written by C. S. Hamlin, Assistant Secretary of the Treasury.

"Treasury Department, Washington, March 6, 1914.

"The Hon. Morris Sheppard, United States Senate—My Dear Senator: Receipt is acknowledged of your communication inclosing a clipping from the Chattanooga Times, forwarded to you by Judge Lewis Shepherd, of that city, with a request that the facts be ascertained from this department relative to statements concerning specie amounting to about $100,000 which the newspaper article asserts was taken by the United States forces near Washington, Ga., from a wagon train dispatched from Richmond, Va., in charge of Confederate troops which accompanied Jefferson Davis.

"In reply I have to advise you that no officers or agents of the Treasury Department were in the vicinity of Washington, Ga., at the time the events narrated are said to have occurred. The cavalry forces operating in that vicinity at the time were commanded by Gen. J. H. Wilson, and from an examination of his reports and dispatches as published in 'War of the Rebellion Official Records' it appears that the capture of Jefferson Davis and party was effected by troops belonging to General Wilson's command. The reports referred to will be found in Series 2, Volume XLIX., pages 653, 702, 719, 721, and 955. 'War of the Rebellion Official Records.'

"In the dispatches on page 719 mention is made of $5,000 in specie received at Washington, Ga., and a prior dispatch (page 703) reports the distribution of money by the Confederate authorities to citizens and soldiers at Athens and Washington. General Wilson from Macon, Ga., June 4, 1865 (page 955), advised the Secretary of War 'I have already had this country, from Florida to Charlotte, N. C., searched for the thirteen millions of treasure previously reported by General Halleck and other fabulous amounts reported by various parties. I am convinced from all the information that I can gather that the entire amount of gold and silver with which Davis left Richmond did not exceed one million and a half; that the most of this was paid to his officers and men between Charlotte and Washington, Ga., and the balance scattered among people he regarded trustworthy. Of this, $6,000 was delivered to one of my officers by Robert Toombs, I suspect the remainder was stolen from people's homes by disbanded Rebel cavalry, assisted by our own men. Every house where Rebels have been in Georgia has been searched. It is also reported that the small sums in the possession of Davis's party were pillaged by the captors.

"Gold and silver coin and silver bullion of the approximate value of $80,000 captured by General Wilson's cavalry was turned over the treasury agent at Savannah, Ga., in June, 1865, and accounted for and paid into the treasury: but there appears to be no information upon the treasury records from which its source can be definitely traced.

"The Secretary of War transmitted to Congress reports on the capture of Jefferson Davis, which was printed as Senate Executive Document No. 13, Thirty-Ninth Congress, second session, and House Executive Document No. 115, Fortieth Congress, second session, but said reports contain no mention of the finding or taking of any specie with the parties captured.

"From numerous newspaper clippings filed with office memorandum it appears that much controversy has existed between former Confederate military officers as to the amount of specie taken from Richmond by the party which accompanied Jefferson Davis, and several of them refer to the movement and subsequent capture of a wagon train with specie, agreeing in part with the statements in the Chattanooga Times's article; but the records of this department afford no information from which the controverted statements of former Confederate military officers can be verified.

"Very truly yours,   D. S. Hamlin,
                                  Assistant Secretary.

This entire story confuses the amount of specie, its distribution and the difference between **Virginia bank funds** and the Confederate treasure.

21. Watson Van Benthuysen Story

As the story goes, M. H. Clark, Acting Treasurer, had distributed all except a small portion of the Confederate treasure. Watson Van Benthuysen had been named quartermaster, Van Benthuysen suggested that the treasure be divided with three quarters going to members of the party and the rest going to Mrs. Davis. The quartermaster showed some greed when he added that since he was a distant relative of Mrs. Davis, he should hold her share.

Clark reluctantly agreed to the distribution, but **stipulated that everyone sign a receipt for the money.** The distribution was as follows:

Van Benthuysen	$6,790
8 members of the party (each)	$1,940
5 Negro servants (each)	$ 20
Davis' personal cook	$ 250
Davis' private guard	$ 250

Van Benthuysen went to Baltimore with his gold. Later, when Davis wrote asking for the money to underwrite his defense, he received only $1,500.

It is understandable that questions about this part of the treasure may have led many to believe that larger amounts of treasure may have also been with Van Benthuysen but the facts simply do not support this theory.

False stories, tales and speculation included in this chapter tend to confuse and fail to separate fantasy from reality and truth from lies.

Perhaps it is time to reveal the true story of the Confederate treasure beginning with the Border Town.

BEGINNINGS

A. The Border Town 1728-1860

Danville, in its infancy, and even during the many years of its gestation period, was being groomed to become the southside Capital of the Confederacy.

Tuscaroran and Morotoc Indian tribes, finding the valley teeming with wildlife and having a pleasant climate, made encampments along the river. Colonel William Byrd's scouting party surveyed the area in 1728, and the phrase "river exceedingly beautiful" was penned in his journal.

A decade later, William Wynne from Brunswick County, Virginia, located in the valley of the Dan and lent his name to the spot where the principal mail route, connecting Virginia and North Carolina settlements, crossed the Dan River.

Eventually New World settlers, like Wynne, became disenchanted with their mother countries. That naturally led to discussions of separation and revolution. In Frances Hallum Hurt's account of *An Intimate History of the American Revolution in Pittsylvania County*, reference is made to the many local citizens who contributed to that effort.

One such unique person was James Mastin Williams. The thirteen-year-old Revolutionary soldier, having attained the rank

James Mastin Williams, Sr.   *Wilmouth Walker Williams*

of private, was a messenger for officers located along the Dan River. A favorite meeting place for this teenage envoy was the north shore of Wynne's Falls (later known as Danville).

Williams' view from there was also a preview as he dreamed about building not only his home, but future, at this site. After the war, he wedded one of the officer's daughters, Wilmouth Walker, and built a house/tavern on the southside of the water's edge. Married October 15, 1784, they became known as Danville's first loving couple. Because Wynne's Falls was a shallow place to ford the Dan, their house became a gathering spot for planters heading north to Richmond. Williams Tavern was filled with war tales exaggerated over libations. Twisting his unique pigtail and rattling on and on about his varied experiences during the war, raconteur Williams kept these voyagers spellbound. One local wag referred to him and his house as "tales, cocktails and pigtails."

Serious discussions also took place. Planters had already determined that the Piedmont weather and soil were conducive to growing and harvesting "the golden leaf," tobacco. Hogsheads of cured tobacco had to be transported to Richmond for sale. The only practical north/south route for delivery of goods to the capital was the great postal road through Wynne's Falls.

Because farmers located on the east and west were also seeking an easier way to get their product to the same central location at Wynne's Falls, the Roanoke Navigation Company was founded. James Graham and John Cole were regular boatmen for the Company, whose bateaux were long, flat-bottomed boats, powered and maneuvered by long poles. Their work-a-day attire included dark loose-fitting trousers rolled up to mid-calf and a white collarless shirt exposing dark muscular biceps. In order to "find the boat", they were always barefooted, even in cold weather. Their bateaux heard the humming of tunes as they glided on the Dan from western plantations and endured curses and groans when they struggled upstream against strong currents from farms in Halifax County.

Little boys watched them from the water's edge and imagined that theirs was a life of adventure. No doubt they fantasized about becoming boatmen as well as leaders of the black community. For some of them, their dreams came true. As the business expanded, four other hopefuls were trained to press their poles in the water in order to transport as many as four hogsheads of tobacco at a time. William Scott and Samuel Short were the youngest and strongest of the boatmen. They were known for delivering their cargoes on time to Wynne's Falls.

Saturday, November 23, 1793, the Legislature authorized the laying out of the town of Danville. Seven years later in 1800, surveyed and numbered lots were sold at auction. In that same year, William Spiller accepted the position as the first postmaster for the newly-created U.S. Post Office. In that turn-of-the-century year, only a few families lived in Danville. Among "those hardy pioneers, who struggled under so many adversities" to build a community were the Wilsons, Cabells, Colquhoun, Townes, Barnetts, Walker, Noble, Spillers, Payne, Keaton, Griffin, Worsham, Doctors Patton and McDonall, Price, Rawlins, Lanier and Ross.

The small population seized upon the importance of education and in 1804 an academy was erected. From those young students evolved men who impacted a future generation in the United States and abroad. One wonders how this could have been possible, since the first headmasters placed so much emphasis on discipline and so little on teaching. Change had to occur.

A decade later, Levi Holbrook, a teacher with fine credentials, was convinced by the trustees of the Male Academy to come to Danville and become its headmaster. The catalyst to entice him to Danville was his inordinate interest in making money. He took profits from teaching, invested them in real estate, and in turn sold that land to tobacco companies for enormous profits.

Nothing materially affected Danville until 1815, "when a spirit of speculation began to make its appearance," most likely advantageous to its commercial interest.

The 1816 Map of Danville's Main Street shows the first lots that were auctioned, giving a cartographer's view of how the little town was organized.

In 1820, Danville was still "a small straggling village" of less than 400 inhabitants. People were attracted to Danville by fertile lands, the Roanoke Navigation Company and business opportunities. It was in this year of growth, that on December 27th the Roman Eagle Lodge of Free Masons was instituted.

"They met early in the day, and dined in a body in the Bell Tavern," a large frame building on Main Street, built by George Colquhoun. Fiddlers were employed, and after 6:00 p.m., they danced with their ladies in "the large festive room" upstairs in the Bell Tavern, normally used "for gala balls".

Records of the Lodge on August 4, 1821 relate that two black men, James Battles, a free black man, and Bill, an indentured servant, received a monetary reward of $5.00 for saving "a gallant horse and gig" belonging to the Reverend Joseph Thomas. Evidently, the river had become flooded during a freshet (heavy downpour) when the horse became frightened and lunged into the water along with the rig.

If the toll bridge could talk, it would have related another instance of the same kind. Mr. Welles, while crossing the Danville Bridge with his six-horse wagon loaded with cotton, felt the bridge shake a little, as it always did with a heavy load. He became very much fretted and swore that when he returned from Petersburg he would "load his wagon so heavily as to break the old thing down." He was as good as his word. On crossing the bridge when he returned, his wagon, very heavily loaded, broke through the bridge and both he and his wagon went down. Another rescue ensued, and the good Samaritans were also rewarded by members of the local Masonic Lodge.

By 1826, "the first step was taken for the erection of a Masonic Hall" on the north side of Craghead Street behind John's tannery. It was a "brick building, two stories high, about thirty feet square." The lower floor was a single large room used for meetings, Hustings court and religious services.

On St. Patrick's Day, 1827 the trustees of the town of Danville made it's very first purchase when it bought a parcel of land "to be held by them the said trustees and their successors to be held in trust as a publick burying ground." So, for the sum of $100.00, Danville bought Grove Street Cemetery from William Linn. One wonders why the first concern was for the dead and not the living. No doubt the ten members of the town trustees were heavily influenced by two of their own, the Ross brothers who were Presbyterians.

"Early worshipers [Presbyterians] met at the Danville Academy building [next to Grove Street Cemetery] where the Rev. Mr. Thompkins had preached over twenty years earlier."

The Grove Street Cemetery essentially became the church cemetery since there was no church building to accommodate the parishioners.

The next year the Presbyterian Church was formerly organized during December "with two new members who presented letters of certification æ James Ross from his church in Ireland and Jane Thornton from Pearl Street Church in New York City." [Mrs. Thornton is buried in Grove Street Cemetery, as is an early minister of the church. the Rev. William C. McElroy, who served as pastor for nearly three years until his death in May of 1837.]

They eventually built a church on Jefferson Avenue facing where Patton Street later intersected. This frame structure was the first church erected in Danville, was replaced by a more substantial one in 1853. About this time a "warm friend of the church," Levi P. Holbrook, gave the church its first pipe organ.

Also in 1833, two Presbyterian ladies, Miss Ann Benedict from Connecticut and Miss Excellence Smith from New York (the same Pearl Street Church in New York City that charter member Jane Thornton came from) opened a Seminary for Young Ladies on Wilson Street [then known as "New Town].

In his vivid walking tour description of Danville in 1829, Thompson Coleman, an early postmaster, alluded to the Masonic Hall, Williams Tavern and grist mill, which undoubtedly attracted wagon loads of shucked corn to the southern shores of the Dan and, of course, it didn't hurt any that flasks of corn whiskey to chase away the effects of the day's ride, were also served at the tavern.

About the same time Williams Tavern was showing serious needs of repair and another inn was built on Water Street. Yellow Tavern was not only a place to get a refreshing drink, it also became Danville's only functioning hotel, located in close proximity to the tobacco factories that were being "raised to keep up with the demand for processed tobacco".

The great influx of people to the town of Danville caused its leaders to seek incorporation, which they achieved in 1833. In an effort to keep up with the demand for lodging, Williams Tavern graduated to a three-story frame structure renamed the Exchange Hotel. (Could it be that the name change was a natural outcrop of the place where so many bizarre stories and innovative ideas had been exchanged?)

The Baptist Church was built in 1836, followed in later years by construction of the Church of the Episcopal and the Methodist Church. None of these three purchased additional parcels of land for use as cemeteries, probably because the town of Danville already had an adequate cemetery on Grove Street. [Danville may have the distinction of being the only town in the United States whose churches do not have cemeteries.]

Families on their way to church endured pain in carriages having hard wooden bench seats. William Ayres came to Danville in 1840 as Danville's first upholsterer of carriages. Those pioneer occupations resulted from the demand created by "sore need."

The Masonic Hall had to be abandoned in 1841 because "the brothers curled their collective noses" at the unpleasant smell from John's tannery. Dead mules, no longer effective in front of plows, still provided leather for the upholsterer.

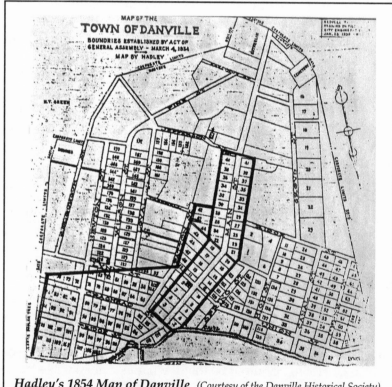

Hadley's 1854 Map of Danville (*Courtesy of the Danville Historical Society*)

An 1849 letter related that 30-year-old tanner James H. Bowe, Jr. and his 49-year-old mulatto assistant, mule skinner Jesse Booker, were wonderfully blessed with a "blockage of the olfactories" which suited them well for their chosen occupations.

Evidently, the Town of Danville liked this site as much as the members of the Masonic Lodge disliked it. By 1851, "the surroundings of the old Masonic Hall and the unpleasant proximity to the odors emanating from Mr. John's factory previous to this time, caused great dissatisfaction among the members, especially on hot summer days. The lodge determined to sell its building and build elsewhere." The Town of Danville paid $2,000 for the Masonic Hall, which they promptly turned into government offices on the upstairs floor where an engineer drew the first complete map of Danville.

Hadley's map of 1854 shows just how much the town boundaries had expanded since Williams Tavern was Danville in embryo.

A spectacular fire in 1855 destroyed the Exchange Hotel, eleven businesses and Levi Holbrook's house. Discovering that the bucket brigade was not adequate to save his home, stingy Levi Holbrook did something completely out of character. He single-handedly purchased Danville's first fire engine for $500. The fire also led a lightning rod expert, John Malcom, to set up shop in the town. Furthermore, the Hodnett Brothers, E. B. and Walden, brick masons, were contracted to build a fire-proof brick replacement for the charred Exchange Hotel. Business-minded and pragmatic, Williams' son convinced his father to make this timely move.

Having a six-foot four-inch frame, coal-black hair and blue eyes, J. M. Williams, Jr. cast an imposing and stunning shadow as the new proprietor, replacing his ailing father, Danville's old visionary who died in 1862. Nevertheless, records of the Baptist Church still found a way to shed light on one imperfection. "We find our brother, Deacon James Mastin Williams, Jr., to be in disfavor with God, and in disrepute with the Church due to excessive drinking of strong spirits." While Jr. served as one of five town aldermen for four years, his younger brother, Robert, operated the grist mill and served as Danville's mayor, numbers two and seven, later building a hotel of his own, the Arlington, up the hill two blocks away.

Diagonally across Main Street, the newly constructed Masonic Lodge made so many contributions to Danville that it would require an extraordinary effort to reiterate all of them. Suffice it to say that "the members put their hands in their pockets" often to help those in need. In one such instance in 1855, they took it upon themselves to erect a monument to Whitmel P. Tunstall "for his indefatigable exertions in securing the charter of the Richmond and Danville Railroad, amidst great opposition". Unfortunately, an untrustworthy member "made off with the funds to build the memorial" and it was never completed. The cornerstone was laid and someone took it away and the last time it was seen, "it was used as a trough to hold water for chickens". George Dame said "I esteem Mr. Tunstall very highly and desired that he should have the highest honors paid his memory, for he was a noble man and did a noble work, but there was no prospect of its ever being done".

Three years before the start of the conflict, Governor Letcher of Virginia appointed Neal's Warehouse a tobacco inspection station. Tobacco farmers from neighboring communities brought their golden leaf to Danville, had it inspected, weighed and sold. Having pockets "bulging with coins", some tobacco farmers enjoyed a couple of days of town leisure ("oratur and women") before returning to country work.

Danville made tremendous strides in growth as a result of the Governor's appointment. It was reflected in the size of government. According to Pollock's *Sketchbook of Danville*, by 1860 the Municipal Government consisted of a Mayor, 5 Aldermen, 12 Councilmen, a Treasurer, Commonwealth's Attorney, Town Sergeant, Clerk of Hustings Court, Coroner, Commissioner of the Revenue. There were only two policemen to "squelch the unbridled enthusiasm of rowdies" who had money to burn from selling a healthy load of cured tobacco and who spent it liberally on "women and brandy".

Danville's 1860 calendar was momentous. Washington's birthday (February 22) was a ceremonious day as women of the town presented a silk flag to the Danville Grays. On one side was Virginia's motto *Sic Semper Tyrannis* and on the other, "Virginia Calls, Her Sons Obey".

With the occurrence of so many significant periodic events, March may have been the most important month of that year.

The Danville Insurance Company (fire, life and marine) incorporated, with an authorized capital of $20,000 to $100,000.

And on the 20th, the State legislature passed a bill to establish the Circuit Court in Danville, whose first session was presided over by Judge George H. Gilmer on the 22nd of August.

Earlier in the windy month, the first through freight car arrived at the Danville and Midland Railroad Depot without having been opened in transit. Later, on Tuesday, November 20, 1860, telegraphic communication was established from the Capital to the Border Town by the Richmond and Danville Railroad Company.

Another interesting tidbit from 1860 was that the value of tobacco sold in Danville in the fall was $574,432 while all other products amounted to only $105,480.

Testament to the new-found prosperity of the town were the five banking institutions including:

The Danville Bank, William T. Sutherlin, President

The Branch Bank of Virginia, Thomas P. Atkinson, President

The Branch Farmer's Bank of Virginia, Nathaniel T. Green, President

The Danville Savings Bank, Thomas P. Doe, President

The Merchants & Mechanics Savings Bank, Alexander Cunningham, President

The 1860's also provided needed educational opportunities for 375 scholars including, Danville's Male Academy, Female Academy, Union Female College and the Danville School for Young Ladies.

Continuing to be headmaster of the Male Academy, Levi Holbrook, was known for didactic skills, discipline and demands. He appeared much larger than his meager frame suggested. This small man had a propensity for intimidating the entire classroom. Oftentimes, he jabbed a "boney finger" in the direction of a student to demand a recitation of the lesson from a book he had loaned overnight. He carried "a stern visage and an ox stick" and wasn't afraid to use either. Most young men from Danville's elite families not only performed well to please their parents but to avoid classroom embarrassment and a possible flogging as well. But that did not prevent them from threatening to get retribution someday. As far as is known, they never carried out their threats.

Alternatively, Danville's young maidens answered to the headmistress of the Female Academy, Levi's wife, Eliza Grout Holbrook, who eventually died with tuberculosis, leaving her husband grief-stricken and in charge of both academies.

The Union Female College was located at the top of Patton Street across from the Baptist Church, on a knoll commonly known as "Baptist Hill." The trustees of the school organized as a stock company and purchased on Patton at South Ridge Street the lot once owned by William Berryman. Following the plans of Nathan Penick, a new college building was completed in 1860, despite financial setbacks.

Additionally, the portals of thirteen public and private libraries opened, having an aggregate total of 5,400 books. To satisfy peoples' interest in public affairs, two newspapers were published, the *Democratic Appeal* (semi-weekly) and the *Register* (weekly).

Craghead Street carriage dealer, James R. McCully, supplied the demand for one-horse buggies, wagons, two-seater surreys and completely enclosed ambulances. Three stage drivers took great pride in going from one town to another and "breaking sensible road horses to the lines." But only Thomas Hines, senior driver, showed the patience and maturity of years to train mothers, fathers and responsible children how to hold harness lines with a sensitive but firm touch.

Road conditions ranged from gooey to bumpy on deep-rutted and dried-mud trails and kept eight wheelwrights busy repairing damaged or broken wheels. Auxiliary occupations flourished as a result of this enterprise. Kinfolk, like the Davis brothers, often entered into related occupations. Samuel was one of sixteen burly blacksmiths, while John B. was a harness maker. Similar services were provided by three saddlers, three wagoners and two harness makers.

The livery stable owned by George D. Moore was the place to learn where all these services could be found. A. B. Chambers operated a very successful draying business and kept two fine draught horses, Isaac and Jacob in this stable, watched over by his mulatto partner, drayman Moses Davis. Outlandish rumors abounded there, some predicting an amazing new form of transportation by iron horse.

As though fulfilling the dream of a fortune teller, on June

19, 1856, the first train pulled into Danville from Richmond. In large measure, this milestone in the town's early development was the culmination of the unflagging efforts of Whitmel P. Tunstall, who fought off his detractors, including Col. Algernon Sidney Buford, and the Roanoke Navigation Company, to establish the Richmond and Danville Railroad Company. Tunstall's fair complexion and thin, emaciated facial features belied resolute square-set jaws and death-defying determination to succeed. Stress from applying purposeful will against formidable odds may have caused him to die two years before the first train entered Danville. Were it not for his untiring efforts to bring the trains to Danville, the town may never have obtained the distinction of being the Last Capital of the Confederacy.

The Border Town was poised for the eventful four years on the horizon.

B. The Company Clerk 1807-1860

A 1788 sarcography tells the story of the trails, settlements and those who settled early Charleston, South Carolina. Among those who paraded prominently into the seaside city were the Trenholms.

Charleston, in the early 1800's, flaunted its own brand of arrogance and elegance. Citizens of the balmy city even walked differently. There was pride in their step, easily noticed even by those with an untrained eye. The Trenholms fit the pattern naturally, both in private and public life.

George Alfred Trenholm was a businessman par excellent, shown throughout his life by remarkable success in varied ventures.

A man with such august credentials must have come from good stock. A tribute to this can be seen in the land holdings, outstanding homes and in the positions of power and influence exhibited by his ancestors. Knowing something about his grandfather, William, and his father, also William, is confirmation of this.

William Trenholm and Irene DeGreffin were the parents of George Alfred Trenholm. There were seven children born to William and Irene Trenholm. The second born child, George Alfred, married Anna Helen Holmes.

Because two of the Trenholm brothers, George and Edward, married two Holmes sisters, Anna Helen and Eliza Bonsall, double cousins resulted.

Further evidence that George Trenholm had keen insight was in his choice of a spouse. Anna Helen Holmes was the daughter of John Holmes, Esquire, of Johns Island.

At sixteen, George Alfred Trenholm left school which he had probably attended in New York and Charleston. Speeches and letters, written by him many years later, attest to a thorough academic background in which he must have excelled. It also provided him with enough mathematical proficiency to land his first job as an accountant. Proof of exemplary performance in that occupation is that he improved his position to clerk for John Fraser & Co., a prominent shipping firm in Charleston. It was in that city on Tuesday, April 3, 1828, that he married Anna Helen Holmes.

Seven years later on New Year's day, George Alfred Trenholm joined the firm of John Fraser & Co. After joining the company, he became a co-partner.

John Fraser & Company achieved financial prominence. Evidence of attaining fiscal fortune is shown in the money that co-partner Trenholm was able to spend on lavish homes. In September 1836, George Trenholm bought property on New Street, choice real estate in Charleston at that time. "By 1840, he was living at 4 New Street."

In 1845, George spent $18,000 to buy a suburban regency villa which had several handsome appurtenances.

While he was a member of the House of Representatives in South Carolina, the Trenholm family lived in a beautiful home named *De Greffin.*

The Trenholm family contributed much to the architecture of Charleston with a proliferation of exquisite homes.

George Trenholm became the senior partner and principal owner of the company. The expanding business had a branch, Fraser, Trenholm & Co. in Liverpool, England. By 1856, all six co-partners had become Liverpudlians.

The Fraser, Trenholm office building is still in existence.

The oldest surviving child of George, William L. Trenholm, was graduated in 1855 with second honor from the South Carolina College [later the University of South Carolina] and left for Liverpool to work for the company.

George Alfred Trenholm demonstrated strong beliefs and dogmatic ideas that he was not afraid to share with everyone, even at an early age. When he was twenty-three years old (1830), he began writing under the pen name of *Mercator*. These articles agreed with the philosophy of John C. Calhoun who held a strict interpretation of constitutional privileges to the U. S. government.

Calhoun's dedication to these beliefs caused him to resign from the U. S. Vice Presidency in 1832. Soon after he led South Carolina into passing the Ordinance of Nullification, eventually leaving the country to war.

Calhoun died in 1850 neither achieving his aim of becoming President nor that of uniting the South.

Trenholm was elected to the South Carolina House of Representatives in 1852.

His great-granddaughter, Ethel Nepveux, wrote, "In 1852, Trenholm was a separate action secessionist, wanting South Carolina to secede by herself if necessary."

Unseasonably hot weather greeted the National Democratic Convention that met in Charleston in April, 1860. The stifling heat was unbearable. Many Northern delegates hadn't been that far South before and were miserable in their layered springtime clothing. Matching the torrid temperatures, sectional differences also flared, and eight Southern states withdrew, including the host state. When the convention adjourned to Baltimore, Southern delegates separated themselves and took off to Richmond. Another election was held to select delegates for South Carolina. Trenholm was elected as an alternate delegate-at-large to Richmond. On July 10, he substituted for John G. Breckenridge, the Southern Democratic presidential nominee. Stephen A. Douglas was the national Democratic nominee and Lincoln and the Republicans handily defeated the divided Democrats.

Trenholm was back in the South Carolina House for a special session of the legislature for protection of the State. The House had been in session since October 12, when the Governor of South Carolina, Francis W. Pickens, asked them to remain until after the National Election. On November 6, the returns showed that Lincoln had won.

At Institute Hall, November 17, 1860, George A. Trenholm made an eloquent speech in which he agreed with "the constitution of the illustrious Calhoun" and further states that Lincoln had been elected "by a party who are against and above the constitution, proclaiming a higher law."

As soon as South Carolina voted to secede on December 10, 1860, Trenholm became a strong supporter of secession.

In her excellent book *George Alfred Trenholm: The Company That Went To War*, his great-granddaughter Ethel wrote, "In 1861, George Alfred Trenholm's name was shown on the voting list for almost every bill," including one "asking for the issuance of $1,800,000 in stock by the state for military defense."

Even then, the monetary affairs of his state government were of paramount concern to him and his fiscal efforts and those of his company on behalf of South Carolina were duplicated for the future Confederate States of America.

John Fraser & Company had seagoing vessels, some capable of transporting more than a thousand bales of cotton from Carleston to Liverpool.

The federal government later claimed that Fraser, Trenholm & Co.'s principals were really South Carolinians who set up the Liverpool branch in anticipation of war. One, Charles Prioleau, became a British subject to help the South's cause.

On the eve of the Civil War, George Alfred Trenholm was "the wealthiest man in the South" and headed up the most successful business enterprise there.

According to great-granddaughter Ethel Trenholm Seabrook Nepveux, it was *The Company That Went to War.*

THE WAR YEARS - 1861 TO APRIL 2, 1865

A. The River Town

While tobacco reigned brightly as king of business, dark rumors of the possibility of an impending war circulated around the river town of Danville. Edward Pollock wrote, "Sensitive and high-spirited towns people clamored for secession, while the more prudent and less excitable agricultural population shrank from the perilous chance of provoking a conflict, who's end they could not see, so long, at least, as the possibility existed that the 'soft answer' and 'counsel sweet' might haply avert the catastrophe." Although the county outvoted the city in the fall of 1860 to remain with the Union (pending the outcome of certain political events), the gallant little town of Danville, although beaten, was not crushed, at which point Danville raised a lofty secession pole next to the fountain in the front yard of John Holland's house on Main Street.

What happened after that is only too well known. The fall of Fort Sumter, caused Lincoln to respond by calling for Federal Forces to put down the rebellion. At that time Virginia was violated by the Northern hordes and became the main battlefield of the Eastern Campaign, as well as the executive offices of the Confederate Government. Since the original capital in Montgomery, Alabama was unsatisfactory, Richmond was shortly thereafter named the Capital of the South. After Virginia seceded from the Union in 1861, Danville and Pittsylvania County "took on a unified stance and helped the South's Cause in any way they could."

What happened to the educational institutions was an indicator of this fact. It was reported that E. J. Bell was among the trustees of the Male Academy who, in 1863, voted to demolish the log structure that was the academy building. Sitting forlornly in the middle of thirty locust trees planted by Hezekiah Pigg in 1850, it was then almost vacant because most of Danville's young men were serving in the Civil War.

Because of the conflict, operation of The Union Female College was "hampered by flagging attendance and lack of money." A Baptist clergyman, William Allen Tyree, who married a relative of the founder, Miss Susan B. Penick, was selected as the first principal of the school. He sustained it through much of the war until his resignation and return to the ministry in 1863.

The Union Female College's originator and some of the Averetts were among the first teachers. Joseph James Averett (Joe Jim), a 5' 11" teacher with blue eyes, light hair, and a fair complexion, was in Company A of the 18th Virginia Regiment for over a year until wounds in his shoulder and a physical disease crippled him. His seat on the faculty was literally a wheelchair, from which he continued teaching the small remnant of students not directly involved in the fighting.

Another interesting story evolving from the effects of the war is found in the incidence involving James Mastin Williams, Jr. In 1864, the lofty hotel keeper J. M. Jr. was murdered by Moses Echols in Pittsylvania County in a dispute over a land deal. Food was scarce during the war years and Echols tried to re-negotiate the selling price of his land because "it had a turnip patch and an orchard," both valuable commodities. When J. M. Jr. reached in his saddlebag for money to pay the originally agreed-to price, Echols mistakenly thought Williams was going for his gun instead. The angry Echols "raised a loaded pistol" and fatally shot him point blank. When caught, Echols turned the weapon on himself and died four days later in Chatham jail.

At 1 a.m. on April 23, 1861 telegraph keys at Danville clattered with the governor's directive. Young men were roused from their sleep by the roll of the drum beat [drummer Austin Dix, a black man] piercing the quietness of the night. The *Danville Register* noted, "at five o'clock were on the [railroad] cars off from the wars ... Thus went forth from our midst, on this mission of patriotism, more than two hundred of the flower of our young men." All in the community rallied around their sons, husbands and fathers.

Col. Robert E Withers
Danville Post Commander

The composition of Withers' Regiment, as it was first called (the 18th Virginia Infantry), was as follows:

Company A: "Danville Blues," Capt. William P. Graves
Company B: "Danville Grays," Capt. Thomas D. Claiborne

Commanding the regiment was Robert Enoch Withers, a Campbell County physician who had moved to Danville in the mid-1850s and became one of the most prominent men in the community. Withers was thirty-nine; and although his experience under arms was restricted to militia service, he was by nature a man wedded to organization and discipline. He was also passionately devoted to the South. Assisting Withers was Lt. Col. Henry A. Carrington, a Richmond attorney, and Maj. George C. Cabell, who had divided his time in Danville between law and newspaper publishing.

Some of the 200 soldiers Danville sent into the conflict "to resist the invader" were listed in the records of companies A and B, 18th Virginia Infantry.

The following listing was obtained from the company's April/June 1863 muster roll captioned June 30, 1863 near Chambersburg, Pennsylvania. There were two companies initially officered as follows:

Company A 18th Virginia Regiment Danville Blues	Company B 18th Virginia Regiment Danville Grays
Captain, William P. Graves	*Captain, Thomas D. Claiborne*
1st Lieutenant, Dr. James M. Smith	*1st Lieutenant, Edward N. Sorey*
2nd Lieutenant, Dr. E. D. Withers	*2nd Lieutenant, J. Daniel Turner*
3rd Lieutenant, James A. Holland	*3rd Lieutenant, Robert McCullough*
1st Sergeant, William D. Coleman	*1st Sergeant, Archibald Pleasants*
2nd Sergeant, James M. Walker	*2nd Sergeant, Samuel S. Grasty*
3rd Sergeant, Stephen A. Rice	*3rd Sergeant, William H. Lipscomb*
4th Sergeant, Robert S. Neal	*4th Sergeant, Harry Wooding*
1st Corporal, John C. Enright	*5th Sergeant, James Fitzjames*
2nd Corporal, Jacob Wolff	*1st Corporal, James M. Murrie*
3rd Corporal, John S. Paxton	*2nd Corporal, James W. Womack*
4th Corporal, Thomas G. Wooding	*3rd Corporal, Lewis L. Vaughan*
	4th Corporal, Charles E. Dougherty

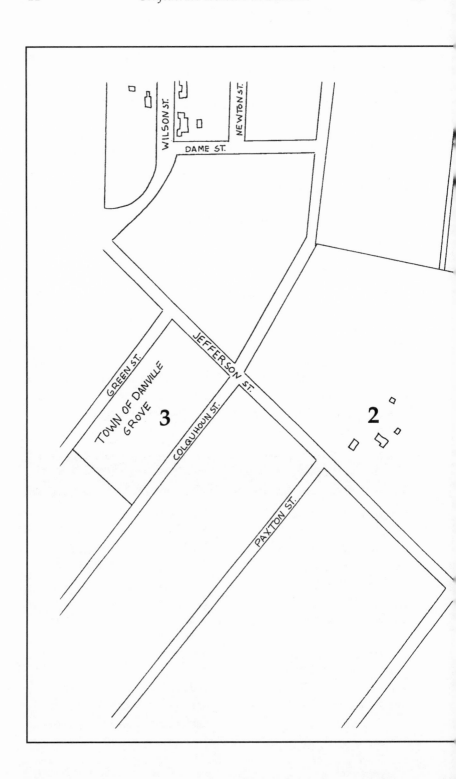

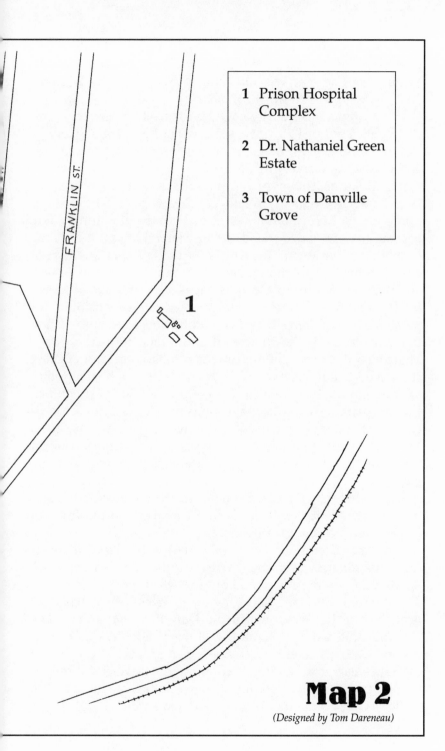

1 Prison Hospital
   Complex

2 Dr. Nathaniel Green
   Estate

3 Town of Danville
   Grove

FRANKLIN ST.

1

Map 2

(Designed by Tom Dareneau)

Company A was organized in February 1841; this company enlisted April 23, 1861 at Danville, Pittsylvania County, Virginia for one year; was mustered into service April 24, 1861; and was reorganized April 23, 1862.

Company B was organized in December 1859; this company enlisted April 23, 1861 at Danville, Pittsylvania County, Virginia for one year; was mustered into service April 24, 1861; and was reorganized April 26, 1862.

Besides those previously listed, there were 192 Danvillians in Company A and 174 in Company B of the 18th thought too old for military service. Perhaps unwittingly, fate became an unintended friend, because later that year during the typhoid fever epidemic, his wife Bettie died. The house was not empty though. A six-month old infant daughter, "Little Bettie", and two sons, John and Mortimer, ages three and five occupied the Wilson Street residence. He accepted the responsibility for parenting his children, giving his "faithful house servant," Nancy, free reins to guide the children through their formative years. That still did not prevent this drayman-tobacconist from feeling compelled to enter active military service, which he referred to as "devotion to duty". Near the end of the four-year conflict, Chambers turned over the draying business to his partner, Moses Davis. After convincing his deceased wife's parents in Bedford, Virginia to keep the youngsters, he became a conscript and joined the Danville Grays on October 27, 1864 when he was 42 years old.

Other than the Blues and Grays, there were also the Battery of Artillery led by Judge L. M. Shumaker and the Troop of Cavalry led by William Mebane.

At a meeting on January 12, 1861 at Neal's Warehouse, the Home Guard was formed. With an initial membership of 47, it was made up mostly of old boys (age 45 and up).

From time-to-time during the progress of war, changes occurred in the personnel of the Danville companies. The Danville units were predominantly town residents: clerks, merchants, students, agents, warehousemen and the like. During the four-year war, Danville's commitment never wavered although her ranks were reduced by casualties at Gaine's Mill, Sayler's Creek and other blood-splattered battlefields.

Away from the sphere of conflict, Pittsylvania County and Danville residents made further sacrifices by paying a Confederate tax levied by the Confederate government and collected by James M. Williams, Jr. until his untimely death in 1864 at the hands of a murderer's pistol. The vacated position was quickly filled by W. B. Watkins, another Danvillian.

Danville contributed to the war effort in another way. "As a depot of stores and ammunition it was of further assistance, as its railroad connections were maintained until the last." At one time "Danville was sitting on nearly two million rations," making it one of the largest warehouses of food for Confederate soldiers during the entire four years of stress.

Alfred S. Roe [9th N. Y. Heavy Artillery Volunteers] on daily trips to the river to get water for his fellow prisoners, passed by one of the warehouses [20 by 40 feet, 2 stories high]. He stated that it was filled from floor to ceiling on both floors "with captured hardtack and bacon". He requested a weekly ration of each for his comrades but was denied the request because "It is reserved for our troops in the field."

From 1863 to 1865, Danville was one of the principal points for the exchange of prisoners and six large tobacco warehouses domiciled Federal soldiers. On the corner of Linn and Loyal, a tobacco factory belonging to Major Willliam T. Sutherlin was converted to prison number six in 1863. Many black soldiers captured on July 30, 1864 at the crater in Petersburg were confined there. This castle-like structure was seen many times by cabinet members, various clerks and even President Davis himself as they made their rounds throughout the town. [The founders of Loyal Baptist Church were made up of some of these black prisoners.]

The large brick tobacco factory owned by J. W. and C. G. Holland at the apex of the hill on Spring Street, on the corner of Union Street had been converted into military prison number five for Federal officers . About 500 prisoners were confined on the second and third floors of the three-story building waiting to be exchanged for Confederate officers who had been confined in Federal prisons.

In December, 1864 five companies of soldiers from Virginia and North Carolina regiments who had been guarding the prisoners were called to the front lines. Their place was taken

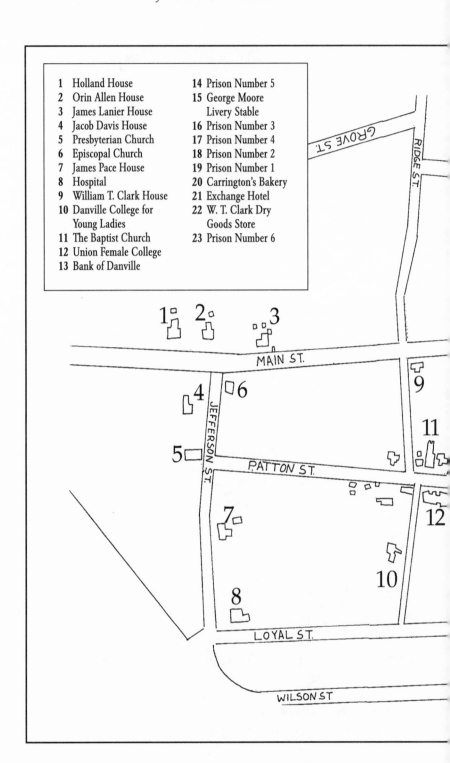

1 Holland House	14 Prison Number 5
2 Orin Allen House	15 George Moore
3 James Lanier House	Livery Stable
4 Jacob Davis House	16 Prison Number 3
5 Presbyterian Church	17 Prison Number 4
6 Episcopal Church	18 Prison Number 2
7 James Pace House	19 Prison Number 1
8 Hospital	20 Carrington's Bakery
9 William T. Clark House	21 Exchange Hotel
10 Danville College for	22 W. T. Clark Dry
Young Ladies	Goods Store
11 The Baptist Church	23 Prison Number 6
12 Union Female College	
13 Bank of Danville	

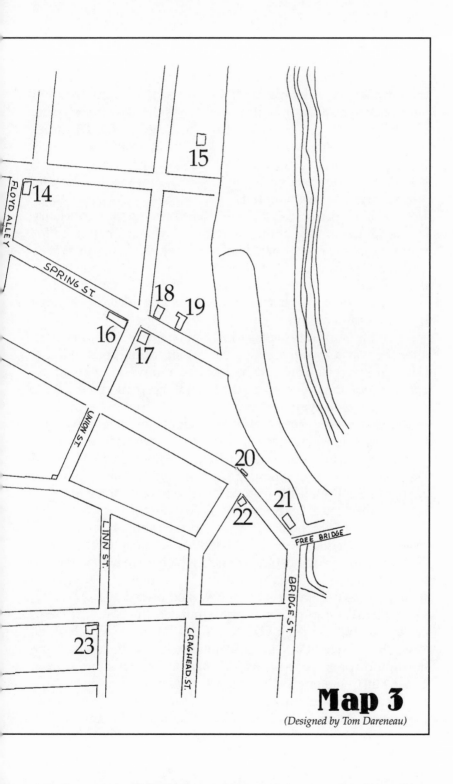

Map 3

(Designed by Tom Dareneau)

by militia men from nearby counties. When the prisoners noticed the lax training of the newcomers, they planned to take advantage of the opportunity and risk a break for freedom. Although they carefully planned, they failed to take into account "the noisy rush of many boots on the two flights of wooden stairs, which was an effective call to arms for the guards." The outer doors of the prison were shut and "a volley from the muskets through the barred windows sent the prisoners flying back up the stairs." Their leader, Colonel Raulston, was killed and no more escapes were attempted.

Union prisoners who were ill were taken to an infirmary on the southern edge of the town limits. They were treated for everything from diarrhea to dementia. Dr. J. F. Fauntleroy served as director/surgeon. He led the prison hospital, consisting of three wooden buildings and four large tents, located on a hillside in a grove of trees between Lee Street and the narrow gauge Piedmont railroad lines.

One of the infirmed, J. M. Thurston (a private from Ohio), after the war drew an accurate *pen and ink* of the complex. Because he suffered from severe diarrhea and made frequent excursions outside, the view of the hillside hospital and even the exact location of every tree became forever fixed in his mind.

In a classic case of medical doctors bickering, the hospital director, Dr. Fauntleroy, sarcastically reported about the "meddlesome and noisy complainings of the sapient Mayor of Danville." According to him, "Hizzoner" Dr. Thomas P. Atkinson, also a physician, foolishly warned the citizens of the town that they may be subject to airborne communicable diseases.

The entire wood and canvas hospital entity received 4,322 cases of which there were 1,074 fatalities—almost thirty per cent according to prison hospital records which were kept from November, 1863 to 1865. [Later, a National Cemetery was laid out, honoring the Federal prisoners who died there.]

Adjacent and in close proximity to the National Cemetery was land owned by Dr. Nathaniel T. Green. A map of the Green Homestead Place in the Danville Clerk's Office shows the house and appendages facing on Jefferson Street not too far from Green Hill Cemetery and included acreage now comprising large portions of Colquhoun, Paxton, Berryman, Stokes, Jefferson and Lee streets. He owned extensive land along the Piedmont Railroad [now Southern] and other large tracts in the town and county. Called Green Hill Cemetery, the name came from the man who owned the land, Dr. Nathaniel T. Green.

During the period of the war between the states, Danville experienced only some of the depletion that the Confederate capitol in Richmond endured. It effectually ended Danville's prosperity which had been gained through the sale and inspection of tobacco. Although Danville suffered anxiety and loss, its position on the southern border of the state kept it from most of the actual conflct.

Some of the problems of diminished resources that plagued Richmond existed in Danville as well but not to the same extent. Since many of the young farmers had gone away to war, their wives, children, and parents continued to plow the fields and harvest the crops.

As Danville's young men paraded away to join the fighting forces, a spirit of camaraderie and community cemented the populace. Merchants and clerks still at home, backed each up other. Neighbors supported neighbors. Friends sustained friends. "And all sought mercy and guidance from the Almighty."

This cooperative pluck enabled Danville's citizens the luxury of not having to feel the complete brunt of insufficiency. Although most foodstuffs were in short supply, the cost of some items were not nearly so inflated as they were in Richmond, where butter was $25 a pound and $6 a dozen for eggs compared to Danville's $12 a pound for butter and $4 a dozen for eggs.

If delicacies like tomatoes, cucumbers and beans were in short supply, there was still an abundance of cornfield peas, corn, onions, turnips and turnip salad.

At one time or another, "scratch bread and sopping broth" graced nearly every table. However, gravy consisted of a thin broth flavored by meat bones or "pot likker" juice derived from parboiling turnip greens.

Precious few had rosy apples to eat raw, cooked or made into fried apple pies. A home-made pickle was a sight for sore eyes. Salads had no oil; preserves had no sugar.

Food products of all kinds found their way to some of Danville's tables, but it cost them dearly. Wealthier families paid premium prices for any cut of meat while others made do with anything they could scrape up.

Some farms had a few scratching chickens, a cow or a lean pig to supplement their meager fare with eggs, churned butter, milk and meat. Lucky was the hunter who bagged a wild turkey for his family.

On rare occasions, when fortunate enough to obtain the ingredients, John Carrington's Bakery and Confectionery at the lower end of Main Street made a batch of thin sorghum candy which was gobbled up immediately by those who heard sweet tooth rumors and had enough Confederate money to pay for it.

All segments of society felt the pangs of wantonness, but none more than the soldiers of the 18th Virginia Regiment. Harry Wooding reported, "We were living upon one meal a day and that a very poor one." They were also victims of "indifferent fare and inferior accommodations" and their "loud complaints set Danville ladies to sewing cots for the men folk."

Twenty-five seamstresses and five tailors were forced to sit erect at their iron treadle and stand sewing machines. The tall Wheeler-Wilcox types in use would not permit slouching as they continued to sew and re-make garments from used clothing. Bolts of wool cloth, easily obtained before the war, became almost nonexistent.

Danville stores, those that opened at all. were manned by eleven clerks and fourteen merchants who opened for business daily but mostly stood around discussing "the evaporated trade and the sparse shelves." It appeared that the only products readily available were ubiquitous tobacco and whiskey.

Since many of Danville's residents were away from home fighting for the Cause, women and old boys had to take up the slack and hold down more than one occupation to keep the town going.

Orin N. Allen was both a "dentist who attended patients near and far" and an amateur architect. Abner Anderson was editor of the *Register* but was educated to be a physician. A. S. Buford was a physician and lawyer. A. B. Chambers was not only a tobacconist; he also was the best drayman in town, He negotiated work for food so successfully that envious citizens begrudgingly said that he had "the best cellar and pantry in Danville." Perhaps the person having the most multiple occupations was Thomas B. Atkinson, who wore many hats. Not only a physician, he was Danville's 6th, 14th, and 19th mayor, State Senator many times and president of the Branch Bank of Danville. Surprisingly, he had still enough time to "put his nose into everybody's business", as one contemporary casually revealed in a letter of that day.

In some small way, enduring these survival techniques helped prepare Danville to accept the notion of being the next Capital of the Confederacy.

By 1865, the population had grown to 3,500 souls and although the ravages of war were felt, Danville was still the hub of what was left of the social and business activities in southside Virginia. The Exchange Hotel was the domicile of the business elite. An open hotel window was in whiffing distance of Carrington's Bakery and walking distance of the major businesses, the railroad depot and the mayoral office.

One who had escaped direct fighting in the war was Danville's mayor, hotel-keeper James McKenzie Walker, who was dismissed from the Confederate Army by orders of the Secretary of War on October 5, 1861. His mayoral office was located on the north side of Craghead Street, situated in front of John's tannery on Water Street. Danville's Town Hall had earlier served as the Masonic Hall and had offices on the second floor. The Mayor's office was the largest upper-floor room, and although not impressive with accoutrements, a large desk, a stuffed chair and three other unfinished chairs spoke something of importance.

Late in March, 1865 and nearby in the Town Hall second-story room, W. B. Watkins, Commissioner of the Revenue, was busy recording those who had paid taxes. Former mayor, merchant W. T. Clark was there with his payment when thin-framed editor Anderson, just having left the train depot, bounded up the stairs and into the mayor's office, clutching a telegram, which he immediately passed across the desk. After reading the message, the mayor excitedly raised his voice and called the commissioner to his side. He slid the chair back away from the table to answer the mayor's summons.

Mayor Walker reached for the piece of rough paper on which was recorded the telegraphic message and passed it to the Revenue Commissioner. Next, grocer and dry goods merchant, Clark, received the note. Revenue Commissioner Watkins and merchant W. T. Clark were recruited to devise a list of men to attend a town meeting. They were also appointed to be messengers, traveling by horseback and carriage, to summon those on the list to a Town Hall meeting.

Craghead Street was replete with buggies, carriages and wagons. Hitching posts had no more room for bridles. Servants remained outside to keep the horses quiet while the invited horde crammed into the thirty-foot by thirty-foot courtroom. The doors were closed tightly for warmth and privacy.

Among the fifty-five persons who filled the downstairs courtroom of the Town Hall were merchants, clergymen, tobacconists, physicians, military leaders, editor of the local newspaper, a farmer, bankers, and other sundry occupations. Seats were respectfully reserved for the oldest gentlemen.

Town Hall Meeting

NAME	AGE	OCCUPATION
James McKenzie Walker	33	Mayor-Hotel Keeper
Charles D. Slaughter	50	Bridgekeeper
Thomas Keeling	43	Plasterer
J. P. Hunnicutt	41	Trader
John Motley Waddill	27	Physician
E. N. Sorey	27	Merchant
A. F. Barker	43	Police Officer
C. Rodenhizer	53	Shoemaker
George Price	50	Tin and Copper Smith
John R. Price	41	Tin and Copper Smith
James Pace	53	Tobacconist
John H. William	43	Tobacconist
John H. Redd	32	Tobacconist
W. S. Flippen	60	Tobacconist
John H. McDaniels	31	Druggist
Samuel P. Witcher	35	Tobacconist
S. S. Bryant	55	Lawyer
Thomas Grasty	55	Lawyer
W. T. Clark	44	Merchant
William Rison	51	Merchant
George Keeling	43	Merchant

NAME	AGE	OCCUPATION
F. C. Parish	39	Druggist
Martin H. Hatcher	38	Baker
M. Frankfurter	40	Merchant
James McCully	45	Carriage Dealer
John T. Watson	36	Lawyer
William C. Grasty	47	Merchant
W. T. Sutherlin	43	Tobacconist
Thomas B. Doe	45	Farmer
Thomas D. Neal Agt	52	Tobacconist
William Ayres	60	Tobacconist
J. R. Fontaine	48	Bank Officer
Julius A. Gray	31	Bank Officer
J. B. Pace	28	Tobacconist
John R. Pace	30	Tobacconist
C. C. Chaplin (Baptist)	33	Clergyman
William S. Patton	51	Bank Officer
Peter W. Ferrell	33	Tobacconist
J. M. Kirkpatrick (Presbyterian)	42	Clergyman
C. H. Hall (Methodist)		Clergyman
Abner Anderson	32	Editor
George W. Welsh	60	Cashier, Bank of Virginia
E. E. Lucians	42	Hotel Keeper
E. J. Bell	43	Merchant
Edward Dandridge Withers	39	Physician
S. W. Gaines	45	Tobacconist
E. B. Estis	60	Merchant
George W. Dame (Episcopal)	53	Clergyman
J. Cushing	28	Railroad Agent
John H. Pemberton	50	Tobacconist
George Jones	27	City Sheriff
James Moss Smith	33	Physician
John F. Cobbs	32	Lawyer
Robert E. Withers	41	Physician
C. W. Watkins		Commissioner of Revenue

The standing-room-only crowd listened intently as Mayor Walker related that the Confederate capital was relocating from Richmond to Danville. He issued an impassioned plea for a new commitment to an old cause. Ten principals were appointed to be a reception committee for President Davis and his Cabinet. Every man, not directly involved in the receiving line still had an important function to fulfill in that every house had to be ready to incorporate into their homes one or more guests.

At the conclusion of the proceedings, the committee of ten gathered in a corner of the room to decide how best to receive the runaway government. Others huddled together and spoke excitedly about the town of Danville becoming the new capital.

At the bottom of Main Street, the Exchange Hotel, a three-story tall brick structure that sported a white triangular flag, also made room for the influx. Owner and widow Bettie Williams, taking time out for respite, sat on the precipice of its round upper floor balcony and pondered what changes moving the capital to Danville would foster.

Danville's **Weekly Register** speculated that Danville would be the new permanent capital of the Confederacy, and residents dreamed of their town being transformed into a great city.

B. The Secretary in Absentia

A parallel story of the impact of an impending war on one individual who would later take a leading role in the Confederacy was being played out in another state. That Palmetto State (South Carolina), crestfallen by the results of the U.S. Presidential election, banded together to take matters into its own hands.

While each city and town in South Carolina responded in its own way to Lincoln's election, Charleston formed the Vigilant Rifles of Charleston made up of the city's first fire company led by Captain Joseph F. Torrent. South Carolina's Governor Pickens accepted the group on the condition of its getting arms.

Fraser, Trenholm & Co. bought a complete outfit of arms and shipped them to New York.

George A. Trenholm
(Courtesy of George Trenholm Boggs)

William Lee Trenholm
(courtesy of George Trenholm Boggs)

Eventually the weaponry arrived in Charleston in February of 1861.

Thus armed, the Vigilant Rifles of Charleston erected Battery Wagner, which prevented the *Star of the West* from reinforcing the Union soldiers at Fort Sumter.

Another ship, *Gondar* (Fraser, Trenholm's ship), brought an up-to-date Blakely Cannon to South Carolina. The big gun was stocked with a supply of shells, balls and apparatus for mounting.

Heavy cannon balls from the new Blakely Cannon were jettisoned across the harbor into Fort Sumter. The cannon and other artillery weapons launched shells, balls and bullets in a constant barrage. Federal forces could not withstand the relentless onslaught resulting from choking smoke and stinging metal. Thirty hours of heavy bombardment was all the Union forces could withstand. Fort Sumter in Charleston fell.

Fraser, Trenholm's ships were involved in the war from the beginning.

Once, an unarmed Federal merchant ship, the *Star of the West'* which had on board 200 fighting men led by Captain McGown, was considering *taking* Fraser, Trenholm's *Emily*. Frustrated because he had no authority to do it, Captain McGown ordered his ship to leave.

After that episode, Lincoln pledged to blockade the southern coast, all 3,400 miles. In theory, his warships were supposed to attack any southern vessel they could catch. Blockade runners frustrated them and made their task nearly impossible. All they could do was watch and complain about Fraser, Trenholm's activities.

John Fraser & Co. was one of the first Charleston firms to send a cargo ship from the port after the blockade was declared.

Fraser, Trenholm & Co. disregarded the blockade and continued taking passengers and goods between Liverpool and Charleston. The U.S. government became frustrated that a stock company from Liverpool was supplying the South with weapons and materials.

Fraser, Trenholm & Co. were accused of "wrongfully using the British flag." They often registered their ships to a British subject, Michael Klingender. It was "one of the tools used by Fraser, Trenholm."

Early in the war the company was appointed a depository for Confederate funds receiving a commission of 1/2%. Fraser, Trenholm & Co. continued to be a branch of the Confederate Treasury. **"Specie and sterling were shipped to John Fraser & Co. of Charleston and to Fraser, Trenholm & Co. of Liverpool and deposited to the account of the Confederate government."**

Regular shipments of cotton (the Confederacy's white gold) were sent to Fraser, Trenholm & Co. to use as a basis for credit for Confederate agents. The company received specie and sterling from foreign governments in payment for shipments of cotton.

In *The Company That Went To War*, it was reported that "Secretly, the firm opened a special set of books, containing a complete register of all the funds the Treasury Department sent."

In the fall of 1862, Trenholm, as principal owner of the company, donated fifty kegs of Mexican silver dollars [(8 Reales pieces) (4,000 coins to the keg)] valued at $200,000 to the Confederate government in Richmond. His donation crossed the Atlantic from Liverpool in one of his seaworthy vessels.

As a further demonstration of his dedication to the Cause, he also gave $2,000 to finance a Christmas party for Lee's troops.

Although C. G. Memminger was officially named Secretary of the Treasury from the beginning, George A. Trenholm was behind the scenes performing the duties of the office. In fact, he was *The Secretary in Absentia*. On July 18, 1864, George Alfred Trenholm officially accepted the appointment to Secretary of the Treasury. Beginning on this date he was not only Secretary in deed but also in name.

C. The Last Days in Richmond

The result of four years of sacrifice and deprivation was especially felt in the capital at Richmond. Life was difficult at best as the last few months of the struggle were severe. Lt. John

Wise explained it, "The problem of sustenance had become serious, even with the rich."

Adequate clothing of even the most prosperous was "simple, domestic, even rough." Poor people wore makeshift garments often nothing more than rags. Those without overcoats rendezvoused in the streets to discuss the prospects of peace "with their teeth chattering, their thin garments buttoned over their chests, their shoulders drawn up, their gloveless hands sunk deep into their pockets for warmth."

Supplying foodstuffs for Richmonders was also a nearly impossible task. Food was scarce and simple, purchased at "prices which sound fabulous." Most families lived upon little more than bacon and cornfield peas. Friends "with ample means were ashamed to invite visitors to share their humble fare."

Hardly anyone thought of creature comforts. "Even the banked and economically screened coals in the grates showed the pinch of hard times." Gas that was produced was of the an inferior quality and purchased at such exorbitant prices. Most people were reduced to the use of candles.

Deficiencies were also evident economically. Observing this problem, Lt. Wise also penned, "Long lines of stores were closed, there was nothing to sell." This was true not only with means of necessity but with items of luxury as well. "Cigars of ordinary quality were $10 each, and whiskey was $5 a drink."

Although facing these impossible conditions, many were still blinded by devotion to the Cause. Thousands of old people, weak from insufficient nourishment, "many without money or employment to provide for present or future" continued to believe the Confederacy would achieve its independence.

This false sense of optimism gave way to reality as one battle after another was met with impossible odds and overwhelming numbers.

By early March, 1865 it was obvious to General Robert E. Lee that he was in a losing battle against superior numbers of Federal forces. About this time, he met with President Davis and held a "long and free conference." He stated matter-of-factly that "the evacuation of Petersburg was but a question of time." The pragmatic side of General Lee was also evident when he discussed how the foul weather conditions made it difficult to move the troops, "My artillery and draught horses are too weak to pull the loads on sticky muddy roads."

Towards the middle of that muddy March, President Davis consulted with another of his Generals about an alternative location for the capital of the government. He wrote, "There naturally followed consideration of the line of retreat."

President Davis' wrote in *The Rise and Fall of the Confederacy,* that he had received from General Hood before the evacuation of Richmond a report presenting his views that if it became necessary for the Army of Northern Virginia to retreat, it should be in the direction of middle Tennessee. Davis allowed Lee to read Hood's report. Lee disagreed stating that "if we had to retreat, it would be in a southwardly direction toward the country from which we were drawing supplies, and from which a large portion of our forces had been derived."

Davis agreed with General Lee to retire to Danville and set up a new capital, at which place supplies could be collected and a junction made with the troops under General J. E. Johnston, the combined force to be hurled upon Sherman in North Carolina, with the hope of defeating him before Grant could come to his relief. The object of this strategy was preparing not for flight, but for further struggle, although his circumstances were indeed desperate.

During the March cabinet meeting immediately following the conferences, concern over a possible retreat was discussed. A question was raised that in the event of retreat, Richmonders may not be able to spend the Confederate paper currency that had become so heavily inflated. There were even fears that Confederate notes would be worthless. Responding to this survival need, all of the cabinet members showed compassion, but none more so than the Treasury Secretary who made a practical move by suggesting that the Treasury exchange Confederate currency for silver.

Following the meeting, Trenholm met with his subordinates in the Treasury Department. He ordered the clerks to begin immediately exchanging silver for Confederate notes at a rate of one silver dollar for every sixty notes. Preparing for the eventuality, pragmatic Trenholm would only allow silver to be used in these exchanges since silver is heavier and bulkier than gold and traveling with it would make a retreat more difficult.

At once, the clerks began to carry out his orders. Sometime during this week Treasurer Hendren smashed the head of one of the fifty previously unopened kegs of Mexican silver dollars donated by Trenholm in 1862. That proved to be a mistake because Richmonders would only accept U.S. silver in these exchanges knowing that they would not be able to spend foreign currency for goods in the event that Richmond had to be evacuated.

The decision to abandon the capital came more quickly than expected. General Lee forwarded a terse note to President Davis recommending that the government evacuate the capital immediately. Because of the gravity of the situation, the courier delivered it to a most unlikely place, the sanctuary of a church.

Many of the worshippers were members of various Confederate offices. One of them, a Treasury Department clerk remarked that on Sunday morning, April 2, 1865, he was seated in the east gallery of St. Paul's Church, Richmond, Va., "in attendance upon divine service." During this service he noticed that someone delivered a message to the President.

The treasury clerk watched as the President immediately stood and walked quietly out of the sanctuary. "As I knew something of the severe fighting about this time on the lines around Petersburg, I feared that there was some trouble, and so I, too, went out of church and down to the Confederate Treasury office." Upon arriving he found Chief Teller Walter Phillbrook supervising the packing of what remained of the Confederate Treasury. Trenholm's clerk, John Ott, had presented written and signed orders placing Philbrook in charge of the specie, bullion, and other property of the department. He was to care for it during its removal and afterwards until relieved by a competent authority. He was to proceed to Danville, Virginia and on to Charlotte, North Carolina.

Because many of the treasury clerks had left Richmond on Saturday night and were not there to assist in packing and recording its contents, Mann S. Quarles, a clerk with the Treasury Department, inventoried the **value of the specie** in the treasure. He reported that the value of the specie was somewhere between $500,000 and $600,000 dollars. [Most likely $523,000.00.]

He proceeded to label each bag, box and keg with the distinctive stamp of the Confederate States of America. Finally, Quarles and his fellow clerks also made the furnace glow red hot by burning thousands upon thousands of "Confederate

banknotes, bonds and papers until everything was destroyed".
[They kept some Confederate currency.]

Chief Teller Philbrook kept Quarles' register and watched
as the treasure was being laboriously loaded by the already exhausted treasury clerks onto the eight, two-horse wagons required to transport the weighty specie to the treasure train. Filled
kegs, bags, boxes and chests added up to thousands of pounds.
Draft horses' nostrils waxed and waned as they strained to pull
the unwieldy cargo to a loading position beside the train.

Since General Ewell
was giving up the defense of
the capital, six Virginia banks
were concerned that they
would lose their specie and requested permission to accompany the treasure train. Their
petition was granted with the
precise understanding that the
funds, amounting to approximately $450,000, would be kept
entirely separate from the Confederate treasure and an agreement was reached with the
banks that Richmonder Judge
W. W. Crump, Assistant Secretary of the Treasury, would
abandon any connection to the

Judge William Wood Crump
(The Library of Virginia)

Confederate treasure and specifically accompany the Virginia
bank funds to verify this separation.

As an added assurance of this agreement, the six reposi-
tories each assigned a junior officer to travel with the treasure.
These bank clerks, who had been roused from their homes to
perform this unwanted duty, were concerned about leaving their
wives in a city that was about to be overtaken by the enemy.
Individually and collectively they insisted on bringing their
spouses along.

Being concerned about the safety of the money, Philbrook
asked for protection. Sixty cadets from the Confederate Naval
Academy were recruited under the command of Captain William Parker and told by Navy Secretary Mallory, "You will go

with the President and Cabinet to guard the gold treasure." He
declared that they were "chosen for dangerous service, because
you are brave, honest and discreet gentlemen."

Parker was unsure how long his mission would last, and
ordered the company cook to prepare only three days of rations.
He and his men were ordered to report to the train station at six
o'clock that evening.

Treasury clerks loaded the precious burden on board the
treasure train while William Harwar Parker and his midshipmen, some of them only twelve years old, stood guard, bayonets ready to quell any false move.

The navy paymaster, Tennesseean John F. Wheless, who
assisted Parker, watched the massive treasure as it was passed
strenuously by hand from one clerk to another. The senior teller
of the Treasury Department, Walter Philbrook also eyed the treasure being stowed into the freight car immediately following
the engine.

One unofficial report stated, "The treasury clerks took
the gold to the depot, where it was loaded onto a freight car
under the supervision of the midshipmen." It is interesting to
note that the Confederate treasure was in the capable hands of
the clerks from the Treasury Office to the train depot. The guards
only assumed protection over the treasure after it arrived at the
train station.

Meanwhile, the Presidential train was being readied for
removal to the new capital. Normally, Burton Harrison, the
President's aide, would have made these arrangements, but he
and midshipman James Morgan had been sent on earlier with
Varina Davis, her children and the three Trenholm daughters,
ages 17, 15 and 13 to Charlotte, North Carolina. Substitut-
ing for him was Executive Clerk, M. H. Clark, who was given
the responsibility of making arrangements for the Presidential
train. "The chief clerk of the executive office, packed Davis' papers and took them to the depot." He carefully listed the names
of those who would accompany the President in the executive
car. [Passenger cars normally had a seating capacity of fifty-five
to fifty-eight persons. The executive car had seating for thirty-
two persons.]

By eight o'clock that evening, all ten cars of the Presidential train were packed with everything necessary for the trans-

fer to Danville except for the people who would make the trip. Soldiers and citizens alike crowded around the train hoping for passage. The top of the train was filled with wounded soldiers while forty-four-foot long passenger cars with a seating capacity of fifty-five were over-filled with soldiers and terrified women. Three anxious hours passed before Davis appeared, accompanied by the Secretary of War (who did not make the trip) and other prominent members of his government.

At once, the shrill signal was sounded and the engine began to tow "the government on wheels," out of Richmond towards the temporary capital. "No man who saw Mr. Davis on that trying occasion," said Postmaster Reagan, "but was impressed with his calm and manly dignity, his devotion to the public interest, and his courage."

By contrast, huddling together like six sisters, the wives of the bank clerks skittishly stood at the station and hugged each other for warmth and support. Nervously they watched Judge Crump and their husbands quickly load the second freight car of the treasure train with the gold and silver of the Virginia bank funds. Hearing the screams of aghast citizens as each new fire broke out over the city, the sextet was exhilarated to see this job completed.

The treasure train departed promptly at midnight. Two midshipmen, with loaded revolvers and government clerks rode in each freight car. (Most written accounts state that the treasure train departed Richmond on April 2 at midnight when, in fact midnight is the beginning of the next day.)

In the darkness, it seemed that an eternity passed before the treasure train departed.

TREASURE IDENTIFIED

So what was in the strange conglomeration which remained in the treasure train that arrived in Danville a short while after the train containing the President, his Cabinet and other government officials?

If the majority of people were asked, "What was in the Confederate treasure?" their answer would most likely be – gold. Yet there was more than gold in the Confederate treasure. The collection consisted of an odd assortment of several items.

Walter Philbrook, the senior teller of the Treasury Department, said that there were barrels ("kegs") of Mexican silver dollars and sacks of American double eagles, gold and silver ingots, nuggets and silver bricks. Also, there were millions of dollars in Confederate banknotes and bonds not listed in the totals. Other things found in the car were 16,000 to 18,000 pounds of British sterling in "Liverpool Assurances" and a chest of exquisite jewels donated by Southern ladies to buy a warship for the Confederate States.

No one can pinpoint when the financial assets or reserves of the Confederacy were first called the *Treasure.* Although they fully understood its worth, the Confederacy, in its infancy, simply called it money. Little Aleck (Alexander G. Stephens, Vice President of the Confederacy), told a friend, "Independence and liberty will require *money* as well as blood." The first Secretary of State of the Confederacy, Robert Toombs, put it another way. "The revolution must rest on the Treasury. Without it, it must fail."

In a letter written to the Editor of the New York Times from his home in St. Louis, Missouri, Monday, December 26, 1881, Walter Philbrook, Chief Teller of the Confederate States Treasury explained some of his personal knowledge of the contents of the Confederate treasure when it left Richmond, Virginia, April 3, 1865.

"You have published several articles relative to the Confederate specie, and although no one believes that Mr. Davis had any dishonorable connection therewith, it may be well for public information and for steeling the question finally, that you make the following known through your widely circulated columns.

I took charge of the specie at Richmond under the following order:

Confederate States Treasurer's Office,
Richmond, Va., April 1865

Mr. Walter Philbrook, Chief Teller Confederate States Treasury:

Sir: As you have returned from the South you will relieve Mr. Wise, Assistant Teller, of the charge of the specie, bullion, and other property of this department, and care for it during its removal, and afterward until relieved by competent authority. You will proceed to Danville, Va., and thence on to Charlotte, N. C. At the latter place you will transfer the specie and bullion to the vaults of the Mint. In case of any emergency which may threaten its safety, you will confer with our agent there, and take such action as may be deemed prudent. The routine of your office is to be maintained so far as practicable, and the clerks who accompany you are expected to subsist on their salaries. By order of

*G. A. Trenholm, Secretary Confederate States Treasury,
Jno.Ott, Chief Clerk.*

Although I have no records of the trip by me, I can say that the amount with which we started was less than $600,000." [Approximately $523,000 in specie].

To be sure, there were gold and silver (coins) specie in the treasure. In the United States before the Civil War began, money was in specie. The dictionary definition of specie is *money in coin.*

Coin boxes were filled with $25,000 in gold coins, made up of five sacks, each one holding $5,000. After the drawstrings were pulled and secured, sacksful weighed more than 15 pounds each and filled coin boxes weighed approximately 77 pounds. Gold specie totaled $180,000 and weighed 636 pounds. A large horde of U.S. silver coins (half dimes, dimes, quarters, half dollars and silver dollars) amounting to approximately $143,914 had been loaded onto the treasure train on April 2, 1865. The U.S. silver alone weighed 8,780 pounds and was not only heavy but extremely cumbersome.

Weightier and bulkier were the Mexican silver dollars (8 Reales) in the cache. There were fifty kegs (4,000 coins in each one) making a total of 200,000 Mexican silver dollars. Each 8 Reales coin weighed .78 of an ounce, and totaling 9,750 pounds. It is no wonder then that Walter Philbrook wrote in his account of the contents of the Confederate treasure, "The bulk and weight of it was in Mexican dollars, packed in kegs about the size of those used for nails."

But what were the origins of the different items found in the fortune?

OLD MINT AT DAHLONEGA.

The Dahlonega Mint, Dahlonega, Georgia
(Courtesy of Dahlonega Mint Museum)

A. Three Branch Mints

Most of the gold and silver coins (specie) found in the cache were minted at the U.S. Branch Mints in three southern states. The Branch Mint Legislation Act of March 3, 1835 that was passed by the twenty-third Congress during its second session said the following:

"Be it enacted by the Senate and House of Representatives of the United States of America, in Congress assembled, that branches of the mint of the United States shall be established as follows: one branch in the City of New Orleans for the coinage of gold and silver; one branch at the town of Charlotte

in Mecklinburg County in the State of North Carolina for the coinage of gold only; and one branch at or near Dahlonega, in Lumpkin County, in the State of Georgia, also for the coinage of gold only."

Twenty-six years later in 1861, specie from these three branch mints became the first part of the coffers of the Confederate treasure. The three United States Mints, at New Orleans, Louisiana, Charlotte, North Carolina and at Dahlonega, Georgia were all seized on different dates in early 1861.

At first, Louisiana did not join the Confederacy. On January 31, 1861 the Committee of the Convention took possession of the Mint in the name of the State of Louisiana. At that time the estimated value of the property there was $591,514.00. The director of the Mint was Captain Johnson Kelly Duncan, who remained in charge.

On March 14, 1861 the first money came into the Treasury "through the Bullion Fund of $389,267.46, in the hands of the State Depository of Louisiana," (This was coin kept at the New Orleans Mint for the convenience of those bringing bullion.) "and $147,519.66, the balance from customs at New Orleans, which sums were transferred to the Confederate Government by the Convention of the State."

No shots were fired when state officials from Louisiana took control of the New Orleans Mint on January 31, 1861. Later, on March 31, the C.S.A. assumed control from the state.

From January 31 until March 31, 1861, the branch mint at New Orleans was operated by the State of Louisiana, during which time $195,000 in $20 gold pieces, and $630,000 in silver half dollars were coined. On March 11, the Confederate government appointed A. J. Guirot of Louisiana as assistant treasurer of the Confederate States of America and treasurer of the New Orleans Mint. Duncan resigned his job as Mint superintendent (He was under suspicion of misappropriating thousands of dollars in specie.).

The convention of the State of Louisiana adopted an ordinance on March 14, stipulating that $389,267.46 in Guirot's hands, known as the "bullion fund," be transferred to the Confederate government. According to old records, there were in the vaults at that time something over $200,000 in bullion, which

The Charlotte Mint, Charlotte, North Carolina
(Courtesy of the Mint Museum)

was coined by the Confederate government, and a good portion of the machinery was later removed from the building by them and transferred to various gun factories in the State. As soon as the bullion supply ran out, the Confederate States of America was out of the minting business.

Although heavier than the silver dollar at a little more than an ounce, the twenty-dollar gold pieces were slightly smaller in diameter at 34 mm.

The following charts show the dates, mintage and values of the coins that were minted in New Orleans and could have been found in the Confederate treasure.

DOUBLE EAGLES
$20.00 Gold Pieces

Date	Mintage	ABP in F-12	F-12 Fine	EF-40 Ex. Fine	MS-60 Unc.
1859O	9,100				8000.00
1860O	6,600				10,000.00
1861O	5,000				8000.00

HALF DIMES

Date	Mintage	ABP in F-12	F-12 Fine	EF-40 Ex. Fine	MS-60 Unc.
1859	340,000	4.00	24.00	80.00	300.00
1859O	560,000	5.00	24.00	80.00	650.00
1860					
Legend	799,000	3.00	8.00	35.00	210.00
1860O	1,060,000	3.00	11.00	30.00	350.00

SILVER DIMES

Date	Mintage	ABP	F-12 Fine	EF-40 Ex. Fine	MS-60 Unc.
1859	430,000	2.00	10.00	48.00	400.00
1859O	480,000	3.00	14.00	75.00	400.00
1859S	60,000	45.00	120.00	440.00	
1860S	140,000	8.00	39.00	180.00	
1860	607,000	3.00	7.00	26.00	225.00
1860O	40,000	90.00	630.00	1800.00	

SILVER QUARTERS

Date	Mintage	ABP	F-12 Fine	EF-40 Ex. Fine	MS-60 Unc.
1859	1,344,000	4.00	18.00	50.00	400.00
1859O	260,000	9.00	40.00	90.00	900.00
1859S	80,000	27.00	140.00	400.00	
1860	805,400	5.00	18.00	52.00	400.00
1860O	388,000	6.00	40.00	70.00	900.00
1860S	56,000	25.00	190.00	600.00	

SILVER HALF DOLLARS

Date	Mintage	ABP	F-23 Fine	EF-40 Ex. Fine	MS-60 Unc.
1859	748,000	8.00	30.00	75.00	500.00
1859O	2,834,000	8.00	32.00	60.00	400.00
1859S	566,000	8.00	31.00	110.00	800.00
1860	303,700	8.00	30.00	86.00	800.00
1860O	1,290,000	6.00	30.00	70.00	400.00
1860S	472,000	10.00	36.00	78.00	600.00

SILVER DOLLARS

Date	Mintage	ABP	F-12 Fine	VF-40 V. Fine	MS-60 Unc.
1859	256,500	110.00	350.00	500.00	1900.00
1859O	360,000	60.00	160.00	300.00	900.00
1859S	20,000	100.00	300.00	750.00	3100.00
1860	218,930	100.00	350.00	500.00	1200.00
1860O	515,000	60.00	160.00	300.00	900.00

The next seizure of a Branch Mint took place in Dahlonega, Georgia.

In Georgia, state officials took control of the Dahlonega Mint April 8, 1861. At that time, George Kellogg was the Superintendent-Treasurer of the Branch Mint at Dahlonega, having assumed his duties in October, 1860.

The report of coinage received February 19, 1861 showed $40,390 working out to be 660 gold dollars and 7,946 Half Eagles.

C. M. Birdsall's book *The United States Branch Mint at Dahlonega, Georgia: It's History and Coinage*, reported that Benjamin C. Pressley was former United States Treasurer at Charleston and later C.S.A. Assistant Treasurer at the same place. He received the gold and silver bullion and coin from Dahlonega on June 11, 1861. The amount received was valued at $23,716.06 and essentially was the same as the report given by Kellogg in his June 26th report as follows:

Gold Ingots	11,975.44
Gold in Sweeps, Scraps, Etc.	517.24
	$12,492.68
Silver Bullion	6,286.38
Gold and Silver Coins	4,937.00
in hand of Dr. of Mint, Phila.	516.19
Assay coins sent to Montgomery	6.00
Sweeps, etc.	730.53
	$24,968.78

The third seizure of assets for the Confederacy was in Charlotte, North Carolina. William Gibbs wrote an excellent account of it in the February 25, 1987 issue of Coin World.

At the time of the attack on Fort Sumter there were only seven states in the Confederacy. North Carolina and three other states had not yet joined them.

When Col. Bryce took control of the Charlotte Mint, North Carolina was still a part of the United States. Four employees were there when the militia entered the front gate and seized the mint in the name of the state of North Carolina.

Although there is no official account of what was confiscated by the C.S.A. from the Charlotte Mint, most reports agree that there were 6,879 gold pieces (half eagles) brought into the Confederate treasure.

One casual report stated that the day each Mint was seized, the money that was taken into the Confederate Cause was as follows:

New Orleans Mint	*$390,000.00*	*19,500 Double Eagles*
Charlotte, N.C. Mint	*$34,395.00*	*6,879 Half Eagles*
Dahlonega, GA. Mint		*$1, $3 Gold Pieces and Quarter Eagles*

The services of all three branch Mints for coining Confederate money were offered President Davis, but it was not the intention of the Confederate Government to institute coinage.

Maybe it would have been wise for the C.S.A. to keep all three Mints operating instead of merely seizing their assets. May 14, 1861 Jefferson Davis signed an act to suspend the operation of the Mints indefinitely. In December, 1861, the Confederacy **had on hand** only $736,468.07 in gold and silver bullion and coin, distributed as follows: New Orleans, $698,832.23; Charleston, $102,565.84; and, Richmond, $30,070. Even an extra $100,000 would have been a welcome asset for the C.S.A. economy.

Estimates are that during its four years of existence the Confederacy acquired about $27,000,000 worth of hard money. By the end of the war **almost all of this** had been used for war purposes.

Executive clerk for President Davis, and later Acting Treasurer of the Confederacy, M. H. Clark, a Richmonder, chronicled in his January 10, 1882 report that had the Treasury of the C.S.A. been $5,000,000 larger in specie, maybe the outcome of the war would have been different.

Perhaps this statement is true. We will never know what may have happened "if". However, suffice it to say that there is a difference in what was in the **Confederate Treasury** during the four years of its existence and what was in the **Confederate treasure** on the day Richmond was evacuated April 2, 1861.

The Confederate treasure came from many different sources including the seizure of gold and silver from its Three Branch Mints. Yet, the largest single form of specie originated from the sale of cotton to Mexican states. These transactions were made in an obscure town in northern Mexico near the Rio Grande.

B. Matamoros Trade

Early in the experimental government, leaders in the C.S.A., especially Robert Toombs, Secretary of State, realized how important it would be to have support from foreign governments, especially Mexico.

Cotton was the most precious economic asset that the Confederacy had with which to negotiate with Mexico. And the 1861 harvest was one of the largest ever, but almost none reached Europe.

Some of the officials in the Confederate government wanted to use the cotton as an impetus to coerce France and England to intervene in the war. So why would the Confederate government foolishly encourage a voluntary embargo on shipping cotton? That policy damaged the ability of the Confederacy to raise money.

Trenholm's company felt that 200,000 bales should have been shipped in the first year of the war. When the Confederate officials realized that his company was correct, they then encouraged them to become blockade runners.

These ships hauled cargoes which included large quantities of munitions and war supplies destined for the Confederate army. A sizable number of harnesses and wagons as well as thousands of pistols, carbines, uniforms, shoes, blankets, and other materials from the Northern states found their way from New York into the Confederacy through Matamoros. Some of the shoes worn by Confederate soldiers were manufactured in Massachusetts long after the War began.

By the end of 1861, most foreign merchants were accepting cotton in payment of goods to be purchased. Arrangements made by Caleb Huse in Richmond consigned all government cotton to Fraser, Trenholm & Co. of Liverpool. In return, that firm extended commercial credit and drafts that could be redeemed in cash.

By 1862 the foreign consuls in northern Mexico began offering specie for cotton, and the merchants from Monterrey to Matamoros quickly followed suit.

Fraser, Trenholm & Co. had beaten the blockaders many times. Their loads of specie received in exchange for cotton made up the largest portion of the Confederate treasure.

In 1862 one of Fraser, Trenholm's ships departed from Liverpool, crossed the Atlantic and sailed up the James River to the landing dock at Locketts. There, sailors unloaded the 200,000 Mexican Dollars (packed in 50 barrels that Trenholm had personally donated to the Confederate government). From Locketts' pier, two-horse wagons struggled up the steep incline to the Treasury Office with their precious burden where it became a prominent part of the Confederate treasure.

The following charts provide information about the coins minted in those specific years that could have been among the fifty kegs of Mexican silver dollars which became a part of the Confederate treasure.

MEXICAN DOLLARS

Mint Mark C

Date	Mintage	Fine	Very Fine	Extra Fine	Unc.
1860/58CE		375.00	500.00	800.00	1250.00
1860CE		375.00	500.00	800.00	1250.00
1860PV		375.00	450.00	700.00	1250.00
1861PV		375.00	500.00	800.00	1250.00
1861CE		375.00	500.00	800.00	1250.00

Mint Mark: Do

Date	Mintage	Fine	Very Fine	Extra Fine	Unc.
1860/59CP		450.00	700.00	1250.00	2200.00
1861/0CP		400.00	600.00	1000.00	1750.00

Mint Mark: Go

Date	Mintage	Fine	Very Fine	Extra Fine	Unc.
1860/50PF		375.00	425.00	650.00	900.00
1860/59PF		400.00	650.00	900.00	1250.00
1860PF		375.00	500.00	750.00	1100.00
1861/0PF		375.00	400.00	500.00	750.00
1861PF		375.00	400.00	500.00	750.00

Mint Mark: O

Date	Mintage	Fine	Very Fine	Extra Fine	Unc.
1860	Unknown	200.00	400.00	800.00	
1861	Unknown	150.00	250.00	400.00	

Whereas the U.S. gold and silver found in the Confederate treasure originated with the three branch Mints, the 200,000 Mexican silver dollars entered its coffers through a cotton trade deal at Matamoros.

Then, what was the origin of a simple keg of copper cents?

3. Copper Cents

Walter Philbrooks' December 1881 letter to the *New York Times* explained that there were not only gold and silver specie, but also a large quantity of copper cents in the Confederate treasure.

In his *Recollections of a Naval Officer*, William Parker related that while he was in Charlotte, North Carolina he had heard a rumor that a large keg of copper cents had been offered to Navy troops which had attached themselves to the evacuating party. He reported that he had only heard about this, had not witnessed it and that if it were true, "it was a very generous offer."

It is not clear what happened to all of these copper coins. However, the following chart lists all of the large cents minted in the U.S. from 1850 to 1860, and if they are still out there, provides the current values of each.

LARGE CENTS
(COPPER)

Date	Mintage	ABP	F-12 Fine	VF-40 V. Fine	MS-60 Unc.
1850	4,426,844	3.00	13.00	18.00	230.00
1851		3.00	13.00	19.00	230.00
1851 Over 81	9,899,700	5.00	24.00	37.00	400.00
1852	5,063,094	4.00	13.00	18.00	220.00
1853	6,641,131	4.00	13.00	18.00	220.00
1854	4,236,156	4.00	13.00	18.00	220.00
1855 Upright 5's		4.00	13.00	18.00	220.00
1855 Slanting 5's	1,574,829	4.00	13.00	18.00	220.00
1855 Slanting 5's Knob on Ear		4.00	13.00	18.00	220.00
1856 Upright 5	2,690,465	4.00	13.00	18.00	220.00
1856 Slanting 5		4.00	13.00	18.00	220.00
1857 Small Date	332,456	12.00	50.00	62.00	390.00
1857 Large Date		11.00	45.00	62.00	370.00

Two other different types of money coexisted with the specie, one definitely in Confederate notes, the other also possibly in paper. One came from British sterling in the form of Liverpool assurances.

4. British Sterling

Sometime between 1861 and 1862 Fraser, Trenholm & Co. brokered a large shipment of cotton to Great Britain in exchange for 16,000 to 18,000 British pounds sterling in Liverpool assurances. Museum curators in Britain are unable to state categorically whether these were promissory notes or actual specie, but their best guess is that they were promissory notes which could have been easily exchanged for specie.

Whatever the case, no further mention is made of the Liverpool assurances by the time the Confederate treasure reached Greensboro, North Carolina. So what happened to the 16,000 to 18,000 pounds of British sterling? That remains a mystery. Could they have been left in Danville?

The Confederate notes that left Richmond on the midnight train to Danville are another matter.

5. Confederate Notes

Trenholm deplored the run-away inflation of the Confederacy in which "printing press productions" were undermining the economy. At one time, there were in actual circulation $250,000,000 in treasury notes.

Treasury clerks "kept the furnaces hot" by burning millions of dollars in Confederate bank notes on April 2, 1865. How much was actually left in the Confederate treasure the day Richmond fell is unknown.

William H. Parker discussed how much he loathed having to guard the treasury notes, especially since with each passing day inflation was reducing their value. At one point he talked about discarding Confederate currency, "We lightened ship as we went along."

Before the government met its final demise in Georgia, Clark received permission from the last Secretary of the Treasury, John Reagan, to burn what was left of the Confederate currency and bonds. On that day, millions of dollars in Confederate bank notes were set on fire in an open field while Breckenridge and Reagan looked on from a respectable distance.

Perhaps the most interesting and least discussed part of the Confederate treasure was a white oak chest which accompanied the treasure all the way.

6. White Oak Chest

W. H. Parker wrote in his *Recollections of a Naval Officer,* "During the latter part of our war, the Confederate Congress passed a resolution, or bill, calling upon patriotic Southern people to donate gold and silverware, jewelry, etc., to purchase blankets for the soldiers. These contributions, made with liberality, principally by Southern women, were deposited in the Treasury and packed in a white oak chest."

Who would have believed that this large, bland white oak chest contained spectacular silver pieces and a magnificent collection of jewels? As evidence of their total commitment to the Cause, Southern women from fine homes magnanimously sacrificed their family heirlooms and their most intimate objects of love.

Those who were privileged to see what was inside the chest were awestruck by the sparkling collection of rings, broaches, bracelets and necklaces, but were more taken by the donation when they realized that it had been lovingly given from Southern women's hearts.

The origin of the contents of the Confederate treasure on the day it departed Richmond, April 3, 1865 lends credibility to the individual portions of the whole fortune.

But what was about to happen to this fortune after it arrived at the new capital in Danville is even more intriguing.

DANVILLE DIARY
APRIL 3-10, 1865

A. April 3, 1865

1. Presidential Train

Captain Given Campbell, "an active and efficient officer" arrived first. It was 1 p.m. He frowned against the sting of the chilly mist that awaited him on the north side of Danville's Free Bridge where he planned to rendezvous with his troops. He rested there, occasionally chatting with fifty-year-old Charles Slaughter, Danville's only bridgekeeper.

Dark-green scrub pines, a steep hill and granite cliffs protected the site that led to the river's edge. The verdant landscape had remained unscathed despite four years of conflict. Danville was fortunate to have endured the war without a single skirmish.

Within minutes his company of twelve from the Ninth Kentucky cavalry joined him. They had been detailed for special service with the President, acting as scouts, guides and couriers for the 140-mile journey from Richmond to Danville. Although fatigued by a sleepless night, Captain Campbell arranged the group into a formation of six rows of two to make an orderly entrance into town.

The impressive parade crossed over the tributary barely one hour ahead of the train bearing the officials of the Confederate government. The horsemen had traveled by a circuitous route. Acting Treasurer, M. H. Clark explained that "the cavalry force did not travel as a rule upon the same road as the party" (i.e., President Davis' party).

Captain Campbell resolutely guided his mount and troops past the tall Exchange Hotel on the right and turned left onto Craghead Street where was situated the Danville and Midland Depot.

Telegraphers from depots at Amelia Courthouse, Clover and South Boston had forwarded messages to Danville's train station giving advance notice of the imminent arrival of the fleeing government.

On Craghead Street a flurry of activity was underway in anticipation of the coming of the distinguished visitors.

Exquisite upholstered carriages jostled with farmers' wagons for a position from which to view, with curiosity, the Confederate entourage. Amidst it all, sharp-eyed local police- man A. F. Barker matched wits with City Sheriff George Jones as they simultaneously spotted the first evacuees of the Confeder- ate Government and made a path for the couriers.

One private letter epistled, "Fine horses, wagons and carriages waited in soft mud on crowded Craghead to transport the Cabinet, government officials, aides and clerks to homes and hotels."

Captain Campbell and his comrades merged with locals beyond the former Masonic Lodge where the Danville Town Council normally conducted it's affairs.

Further down the street, on the left at the Danville & Midland Railroad Depot, a crowd of onlookers were on the street ogling town legislators, who were leaning against empty bar- rels, not saying a word but "quietly pondering the future". Oth- ers were pacing up and down the raised wooden platform, in animated conversation. All were waiting for the Presidential train to arrive.

Two of the saddlebags of Danville's citizens were "freely opened and refreshing sips of brandy were offered" to the scout-

Danville and Midland Depot
(From Sketchbook of Danville, 1885 by Edward Pollock)

Trestle Bridge Opening   *(David Collins, photographer)*

ing party. Tobacconists brought samples of their best chewing tobacco, aromatic cigars and small tins of snuff, which they had hoarded for the more distinguished guests.

Captain Campbell exchanged a few private greetings with Mayor Walker and then explained that the train was more than one hour from Danville, allowing time for a few final arrangements if needed.

Prediction graduated to reality when a chugging, blurred engine emerged from the gray mist into focus. Arched over the Dan River the iron trestle railroad bridge, supported by stacked massive stone pillars in the water, waited patiently to accept the august assembly.

As it slowed to a halt at the depot the Presidential Train engine, Charles Seddon, moaned and gave a giant shush, as though demanding that the expectant throng show some quiet respect for the President of the Confederate States of America. The spectacular event was recorded without fanfare, "The same day Davis entered Danville without unpleasant incident."

The engine of the Presidential Train and the ten cars that followed it had departed from the Danville and Midland Depot in Richmond precisely at 11:00 P.M. on Sunday, April 2. Because the narrow gauge lines were in poor condition and individual cars needed attention along the way, the 140-mile journey to

Danville required sixteen worrisome and tedious hours. Disappointments and delays, meshed with dashed hopes, prevented Davis and his government from reaching Danville until 3:00 P.M. on April the third. The ramshackle and rotted floor of one overloaded car collapsed and some of the passengers fell to their deaths underneath the wheels of the train, necessitating a quick, but sad, burial near the tracks. [The dead were all soldiers from Georgia.]

Helen Holmes Trenholm
(Courtesy of Morgan Goldbarth)

Not only had Given Campbell's troops signaled the impending arrival of some of the stars of the Confederacy, they were punctuated by other, earlier locomotives pulling cars loaded with baggage and clerks, symbols of an ongoing government.

In the Presidential car were thirty men and one woman. Various accounts hint that the following persons shared the same solemn space . . .

PRESIDENTIAL CAR

President Jefferson Davis	Col. Frank R. Lubbock
Col. John Taylor Wood	Col. William Preston Johnston
Judah P. Benjamin	Stephen R. Mallory
George A. Trenholm	Anna H. Trenholm (only woman)
M. H. Clark	John Hendren
L. E. Harvie	Rev. Hoge
Jules St. Martin	Samuel Cooper
Dr. A. Y. P. Garnett	Robert G. Kean
Senator Clement Clay	Captain Wood
A. G. Cantley	S. Brittain
James Miller	J. B. MacMurdo
W. R. Bringhurst	Clay Stacker
General Braxton Bragg	John H. Reagan
John Ott	George Davis
Spencer (Davis' servant)	(Unknown Man) Possibly D. F. Kenner
(Unknown Man)	

Anna Helen Holmes Trenholm, wife of the Treasurer, was the only woman among thirty men. The peach brandy which she took along for her husband, made a big hit with everybody.

President's Staff in Danville
(William P. Johnston, F.R. Lubbock & John Taylor Wood)
(The Library of Virginia)

As they disembarked from the train, Trenholm and his wife were put in a sideless cart after trying to walk with red clay oozing over their shoe tops. Then an ambulance arrived for them in the soggy surface. When the horses lunged forward to extract the thin wheels from their gooey grip, the jerking motion caused Trenholm to vomit violently.

Abner Anderson, editor of the seventeen-year-old Danville Register, hurried from the Main Street newspaper offices to meet the presidential train at the depot, nearly tripping down the dilapidated stairs in the process. He made reporter's notes of the proceedings and returned to the newspaper office to record the momentous occasion for the newspaper.

The presidential train remained on the main track for three hours while hoards of evacuees, clerks, officials and the president disembarked. Other things that were unloaded included some office equipment and supplies, horses belonging to various officials and even the contented presidential cow.

In all the flutter of activity around the Presidential train, no one had the time, nor the inclination, to notice that other activities were taking place.

It was nearly 6:00 in the evening before the presidential train was empty of its contents. Conductor William D. Cheatham supervised the backing up of the Presidential car as it pulled into the number four siding.

2. Committee of Ten

Some one referred to it as "stoned silence"; another, "rapt attention" when describing the mood of the all male gathering to discuss the moving of the Confederate capital from Richmond to Danville.

At this town meeting held the prior evening on the lower floor of Danville's Town Hall, the mayor appointed a reception committee, made up of the mayor, the town council and the Committee of Ten.

Captain William T. Clark	C. W. Watkins
Rev. C. H. Hall	Peter W. Ferrell
Rev. John M. Kirkpatrick	Edward N. Sorey
Rev. Charles Crawford Chaplin	Dr. James M. Smith
William Ayres	Dr. John M. Waddill

Cabinet Members in Danville
(J.P. Benjamin, S.R. Mallory & J. Reagan)
(The Library of Virginia)

Edward Pollock wrote in *The Sketchbook of Danville*, "He was met by a committee of citizens, headed by Major W. T. Sutherlin, at that time Chief Quartermaster of the Danville Post." First to welcome President Jefferson Davis with a handshake was James McKenzie Walker, Danville's hotel-keeper/mayor followed immediately by W. T. Sutherlin. Captain Clark (grocer) was next in line, followed by 300-pound Baptist preacher Rev. Charles Crawford Chaplin, mainly because he was so large no one could get around him. Linn Street Methodist minister, Rev. C. H. Hall, presented his signature firm handshake to the President. Sixty-year-old tobacconist, Willliam Ayres "enthusiastically welcomed the entire cabinet, as well as the President." Others on the crowded, rough-hewn runway forming the residue of the reception committee were C. W. Watkins, Peter W. Ferrell, Edward N. Sorey and physicians James Moss Smith and John Motley Waddill.

Despite "the inordinate number of muddy boots filling every nook and cranny of the platform floor" of the Craghead Street depot, somehow Episcopal clergyman Dr. George W. Dame and tobacconist-councilman Christopher G. Holland managed to find their own place to stand.

Following the President out of his car were members of the President's Cabinet (with the exception of Secretary Trenholm), George Davis, Attorney General, who ducked his head to keep from striking the exit doorway, black-bearded Postmaster General John H. Reagan, who "did nothing to hide his gruff Texas background," Judah P. Benjamin who carried a beautifully carved cane in one hand and nursed his ever-present cigar in the other, and Secretary of the Navy Stephen Russell

The Ann Benedict House
(From Sketchbook of Danville. 1885 by Edward Pollock)

Mallory. Because he was suffering with neuralgia, Secretary of the Treasury, George Alfred Trenholm and his wife Anna, were the last to leave the Presidential car. Mercifully this was so because the first thing Secretary Trenholm did once his feet hit the ground, was to throw up. (Could it be that the large quantities of fine peach brandy imbibed on the train to alleviate pain contributed to the regurgitation?)

3. The Ann Benedict House

It had been decided at the Town Meeting, as reported by Edward Pollock in 1885, "The Benedict House, a large brick building on Wilson Street, long since demolished, was assigned as Government headquarters and Executive offices."

Miss Excellence Smith and Miss Ann Benedict formerly operated it as a Seminary for Young Ladies. Now it was a large unoccupied two-story building at 142 Wilson Street. Inside the structure was an adequate kitchen, dining room, office space for the various departments and several upstairs bedrooms where many of the government officials stayed during the week.

In President Davis' memoirs he wrote that, "The different departments resumed their routine labors." He later recorded that at Danville he "found several Bureaus of the War Department, with other departments of the Confederate Government organized for work in regular quarters in the town."

The executive secretary, M. H. Clark, had started the work of organizing the Executive Offices: and the President was planning military activities with apparent calm and confidence.

4. Sutherlin Mansion and Other Homes

Davis said, "Though the occupation of Danville was not expected to be permanent, immediately after arriving there, rooms were obtained."

Major Sutherlin invited President Davis, Secretary Mallory and Secretary Trenholm and his wife as well as the three members of the President's personal staff to stay together at his commodious plantation house situated where the town ended on Main Street. President Davis later wrote, "They cordially gave us an old Virginia welcome, and with one heart contributed in every practicable manner to cheer and aid us in the work in which we were engaged."

Other government officials stayed at the Benedict House on Wilson Street. The town's hotels, the Exchange and Tunstall House, were "filled with government lackeys."

Those with more spacious accommodations were also more than generous with their hospitality. The large homes of G. T. Pace on Jefferson Street, Colonel Algernon Sidney

W.T. Sutherlin
(The Library of Virginia)

Buford on Main Street, George Ayres on Main Street (formerly Jacob Davis' house), James Lanier on Main Street, and W. T. Clark on Main Street provided sleeping quarters for multiple members of evacuees.

Local physician, T. D. Stokes, who lived quietly in a gothic style cottage on Pine Street, offered accommodations for a single guest, but no one knows who it was.

William T. Clark House
(Courtesy of The Ladies Benevolent Society)

Benjamin found himself without a place to sleep, but the Rev. Hoge invited him to stay with him at the Wilson Street home of John M. Johnston, cashier at the Bank of Danville.

Lesser accommodations were those provided by the men for themselves. The twelve scouts and couriers led by Given Campbell bivouacked in tents. The President's guard, made up of three one-armed officers, Captain Coe, Lieutenant Brown and Lieutenant Dickinson and nine additional disabled soldiers, pitched their tents on the Sutherlin property. General George G. Dibrell, a gallant Tennessean, led the cavalry escort which was really a small division made up of William's Brigade, Dibrell's Brigade and Hewitt's Battery and set up a tent city on the outskirts of town.

After Major William T. Sutherlin offered his home to Davis and his staff, Mayor James Walker and the town council gave him a warm welcome and escorted him to the large Sutherlin home "built with the fortune he had made in tobacco before the war." Davis and members of his cabinet were served their first hot meal since leaving Richmond.

Davis wrote a letter to Varina before retiring Monday evening to tell her that he had escaped the capital safely and that he had reached the new southside capital of Danville, just barely within the border of Virginia. He explained, "I am unwilling to leave Virginia."

In his memoirs, Davis wrote, "The design, as previously arranged with General Lee, was that if he should be compelled to evacuate Petersburg, he would proceed to Danville, make a new defensive line of the Dan and Roanoke Rivers and make a combined attack (with Johnston) upon Sherman." If that failed, Davis wrote, "It was expected that reviving hope would bring reinforcements to the army, and Grant being then far removed from his base of supplies, and in the midst of a hostile population, it was thought we might return, drive him from the soil of Virginia, and restore to the people a government deriving its authority from their consent."

Afterwards he rode by horseback to the depot where he met telegrapher, William M. Tredway, to make inquiries as to the whereabouts and condition of Lee and his army, but could learn nothing.

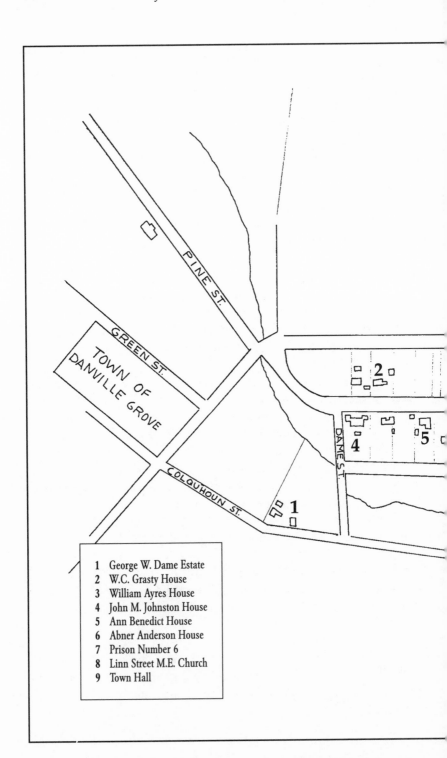

1 George W. Dame Estate
2 W.C. Grasty House
3 William Ayres House
4 John M. Johnston House
5 Ann Benedict House
6 Abner Anderson House
7 Prison Number 6
8 Linn Street M.E. Church
9 Town Hall

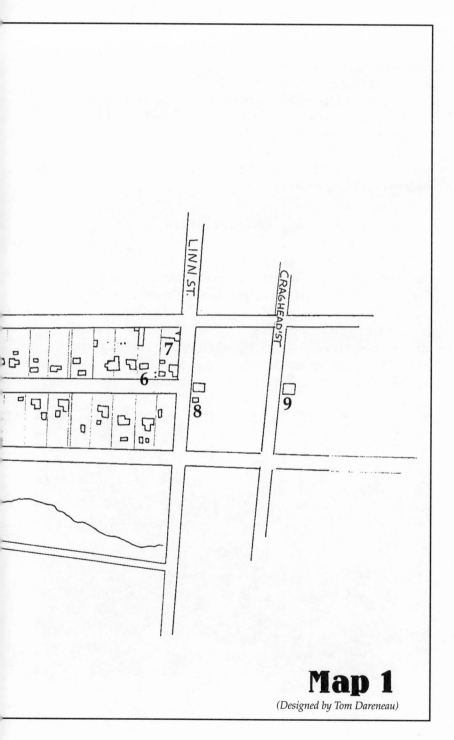

Map 1

(Designed by Tom Dareneau)

Edward Pollock's 1885 *Sketchbook of Danville* related, "Hospitable homes had thrown open their doors to the distinguished visitors and their attendant officials and scarcely a home was without one or more guests."

Some of the other homes notably opened to government officials were those of Colonel Robert Enoch Withers (Commander of the Danville Post), Abner Anderson, William S. Patton, J. M. Johnston, J. R. Pace, W. H. Wooding, William Ayres, Colonel W. C. Grasty, J. J. Crews and Mrs. M. E. Owens, all residences situated on Wilson Street.

5. Treasure Train

No fanfare heralded the appearance of the treasure train that haltingly inched its way across the trestle one hour after the Confederate officials arrived and made a right turn onto siding number two.

This particular siding had been chosen for several laudable reasons. The end of siding number two was in an elevated position at Linn Street. Due to incessant rainy conditions during the winter and early spring, the ground had become a quag-

Siding No. 2   *(David Collins, photographer)*

mire. The treasure train was extremely heavy because the immense amount of "hard money" (specie) exceeded eleven tons. The other three sidings, situated on lower ground would not support the weighty burden of such excessive proportions over an indeterminate period.

Gray overcast skies and an early dusk helped to mask the coming of the treasure train that quietly lumbered through the fine mist to Linn Street. The distance between Linn Street to Craghead Street on siding number two was limited. The nose of the engine rolled quietly to a stop, followed in sequence by the two freight cars holding the Confederate treasure and the Virginia bank funds as well as three passenger cars.

Nearby on the main track at the depot, the Presidential car continued to occupy center stage. Workers were struggling with bulky items, removing them to places where they were needed, guided and directed by clerks and lackeys familiar with the workings of the government in perpetuity.

Back on the treasure train, Walter Philbrook pushed aside one of the guards and peered out through the dusty window on the door of the first freight car. Dirt and grime blurred his vision until he opened the door to fresh air and a multitude of middies who had disembarked the passenger cars and were intent on protecting the contents of the treasure cars.

Although enjoying the confidence placed in him by Secretary Trenholm, Philbrook nevertheless was exhausted from a journey that proved to be a test of physical endurance. Yet, his work had only begun. How would he handle the responsibility of caring for more than $500,000 in specie? Would he be able to withstand the rigors of watching over the bulky and wieldly cache?

W. H. Parker had been told by W. H. Philbrook that the bulk and weight of the Confederate treasure was in Mexican dollars, packed in kegs about the size of those used for nails. His middies, in their conversations, referred to the Confederate treasure as "things". He saw the boxes containing the "things" many times in the weary thirty days he had it under his protection, but, he wrote, **"he never saw the coin."** (How interesting to note that he never mentioned seeing kegs either.)

In his *Recollections of a Naval Officer* Parker searched his memory for the names of the Treasury officials who traveled with

him. Maj. William D. Nutt,
chief clerk of the Treasury
office (who previously held
that position with the
United States Treasury);
Peter Wise and his wife, a
daughter of Major Nutt, all
of Alexandria, Va., James G.
Bain and R. T. K. Bain and
John Branham, of Ports-
mouth; Henry Fuhri, of
Donaldsonville, La., and
his bride of a few days, nee
Jones, of Petersburg and
half a dozen other treasury
clerks. [He was probably
referring to Walter
Philbrook and Mann S.
Quarles as well as others.]

LIEUTENANT COMMANDER WILLIAM HARWAR PARKER,
CONFEDERATE STATES NAVY.

W.H. Parker
(The Library of Virginia)

Also on board were Judge W. W. Crump, who had been
placed in charge of the nearly $450,000 in specie from Virginia
Bank deposits and a teller from each of those banks, "neither of
which wanted to go," and these same clerks' wives.

6. Guards

Walter Philbrook noted, "We were accompanied from
Richmond to Danville by some of the naval officers and midshipmen from the school ship *Patrick Henry* as a guard."

As soon as the treasure train came to rest, W. H. Parker
posted four guards at separate locations along siding two. Their
muskets and bayonets "at the ready," each was ordered to halt
anyone from approaching the train without proper authoriza-
tion.

The rest of the *middies* were directed to construct a tent
city among the pine trees on the Tunstall property immediately
in front of the treasure train engine. One of the guards, Midshipman R. H. Fleming, penned, "The next day we reached Danville,

and our train stood on the track not far from the depot, and our encampment was in a grove not far from the train." Lt. Parker confirmed that the midshipmen bivouacked near the railroad station. Due to heavy rains, their encampment was in an elevated position on the south side of Lynn Street. (Then spelled Linn Street)

Lieutenant Parker's tent was raised first. It was positioned directly across the street from the train engine where he and his charges could observe the exchange of silver for Confederate currency.

Because "clouds covered the light of the moon" darkness was full when the cloth and canvas community was ready for occupancy. Attending to the mundane matters of moving into their new quarters, neither Lieutenant Parker nor the midshipmen [guards] assisted in the unloading of certain portions of the specie from the first freight car.

Lt. Parker later verified that they did not unpack the treasure from the cars at Danville, *"except that [portion] taken for the use of the Government at the time. How much was taken, or for whom it was taken, I never knew – it was not my business to inquire."*

7. At The Station

When the treasure train came to a rest on siding number two, many of the clerks and their wives applauded their successful escape from the capital and the mood was one of jubilation and gaiety. After the tents had been raised, some of them danced around the campfires, in obvious celebration of their successful escape from Richmond.

While the tent city was being set up, W. H. Parker could not help but be aware that many of the clerks, including Philbrook, continued to laugh and joke nervously about their new-found freedom, temporarily forgetting the seriousness of the moment.

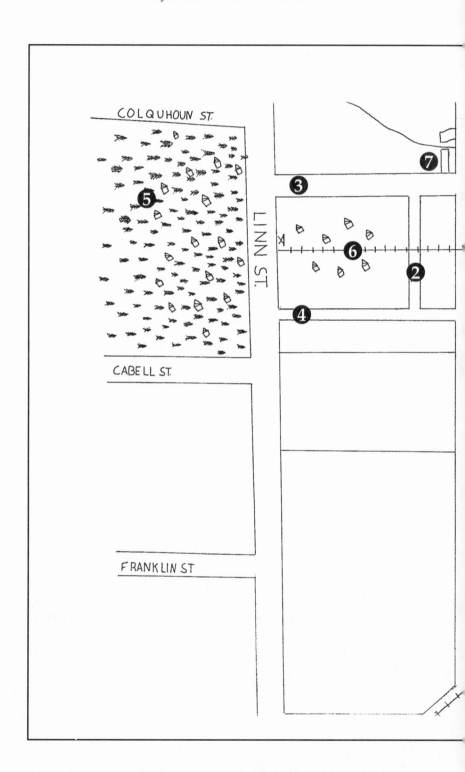

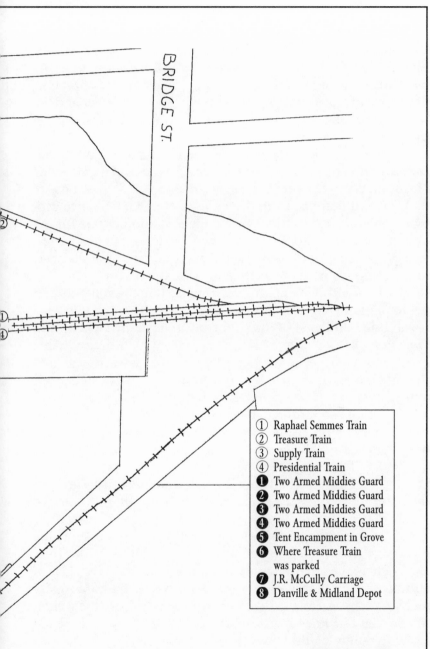

8. Separation

One account stated, "The Confederate Treasury had been divided, half [the gold] being stored in the Bank of Danville, the rest remaining on the train under the guard of the midshipmen." This was only partly correct because all of the U.S. silver and the one opened keg of Mexican silver dollars was all of the specie that remained on the train.

Secretary Trenholm wanted the unopened kegs of Mexican silver dollars to be kept in the Treasury Office in the Benedict House on Wilson Street while he decided how best to dispose of it. He asked Secretary Mallory to instruct W. H. Parker to provide a guard for the Bank of Danville and another one for the Treasury Office. Parker selected two of his best and brightest midshipmen for the duty and sent them on to their separate posts in the company of the treasure they were to guard.

In order to maintain secrecy regarding the contents and movements of the treasure, Secretary Trenholm ordered his trusted aide William D. Nutt to borrow a substantial wagon and two strong horses. Major Nutt himself went to the livery stable owned by George Moore where he took possession of two draught horses (Isaac and Jacob) owned by A. B. Chambers and a sturdy wagon. He returned to the treasure train on Linn Street and instructed some of the treasury clerks to remove the gold of the Confederate treasure from the first freight car and load it onto the wagon. The gold was then transferred to the vault of the Bank of Danville for storage.

After the gold had been unloaded and placed securely in the vault, the wagon returned to the treasure train to retrieve another specific part of the bounty.

It took the two-horse wagon four trips to transport the forty-nine unopened kegs of Mexican silver dollars to the Treasury Office. In order to conceal the treasure from the view of curious citizens, a tarpaulin was stretched over the cargo. Major Nutt, a farmer from earlier days, confidently drove the wagon up the slight incline to its destination. Other treasury clerks assisted in removing the heavy kegs to one corner of the spacious room in the Confederate Offices especially selected to serve as the Treasury Office. Nearly five tons of silver (9,555 pounds) had been removed from the first freight car.

U.S. silver dollars, half dollars, quarters, dimes, half dimes and nickels now shared space on the first freight car with Confederate notes and a large white oaken chest. The fortune that arrived on Monday afternoon had been significantly reduced by nightfall.

B. April 4, 1865

1. Defense of the New Capital

Tuesday was filled with enormous tasks and attendant frustrations. Davis awoke to find there was no word from Lee despite continuous anxious inquiries. Most of the telegraph lines around Danville had been cut, severely limiting communication.

Rising to the song of a mockingbird, the President found much to do in his new capital. He expected to be able to establish his government there more or less securely for Lee to be able to make a junction with Johnston and interpose the combined army between Danville and Ulysses Grant. The city seemed defensible, and one of Davis' first acts was to assign engineer A. C. Rives the task of surveying the city's defenses to make recommendations on further works needed.

Admiral Raphael Semmes and 400 crewmen from the scuttled James River flotilla arrived unexpectedly in the morning.

Because it was necessary to keep the main railroad line clear for the North/South trains, Semmes, officers and men of the James River squadron were directed into the number one siding. After the train settled they were ordered to "Stand by!" until further orders from Admiral Semmes. The Admiral borrowed a horse and rode directly to the Sutherlin Mansion to receive orders from the President.

It had taken a considerable amount of ingenuity, courage and bravery to accomplish his escape from Richmond, especially since he had brought four-hundred men with him. Elated at the nearly impossible accomplishment for which he had single-handedly been responsible, he surely expected President Jefferson Davis to honor him with adulation. Imagine his disappointment and frustration when all the thanks he got was that the President immediately commissioned him a brigadier gen-

eral, a reduction in rank. He was further insulted when his crewmen were converted into an artillery brigade. Semmes was given
the thankless job of directing the Danville defenses and scour-
ing the countryside for food and supplies for Lee's army.

2. Wilson Street Connection

Early the morning of April 4 Davis called a meeting with
all of his cabinet present. They discussed the details of setting up
their government offices in the spaces available. Davis made it
clear that he hoped this would be a temporary location, but still
they all must go on with their work as though it would be forever.

Uneasy, lest his work be interfered with by wandering
bands of Federal troops, but reassured by promises of a proper
guard, Davis wrote to General Beauregard: "The cavalry you
ordered here [Danville] will be of special value at this time, and
with the infantry en route will probably serve the immediate
necessity. Have sent courier to General Lee, from whom I have
no communication."

3. The Proclamation

Later that morning the President called the Cabinet members together at the Sutherlin home to discuss the difficult task
of composing a proclamation to hearten the people for renewed
and persistent resistance. Actually, Benjamin did most of the
writing because he had such a poetic way of expression. Davis
added only an occasional phrase or made a suggestion. About
noon, Benjamin took the proclamation to the office of the *Weekly
Register* and handed the document to Editor Abner Anderson.
Benjamin told Anderson, "There are some erasures and interlin-
eations in this. Let me have some paper and I will write a clear
copy for your printer." Anderson printed the proclamation as a
broadsheet and also as an extra edition of the newspaper.

*It would be unwise, even if it were possible, to conceal the
great moral as well as material injury to our cause that must
result from the occupation of Richmond by the enemy. It is
equally unwise and unworthy to us, as patriots engaged in a
most sacred cause, to allow our energies to falter, our spirits to*

grow faint or our efforts to become relaxed under reverses, how-ever calamitous . . . it is for us, my countrymen, to show by our bearing under reverses how wretched has been the self-deception of those who have believed us less able to endure mis-fortune with fortitude than to encounter danger with courage. We have now entered upon a new phase of the struggle, the memory of which is to endure for all ages and to shed an in-creasing luster upon our country. Relieved from the necessity of guarding cities and particular points, important but not vital to our defense; with an army free to move from point to point and strike in detail the garrisons and detachments of the en-emy; operation in the interior of the country, where supplies are more accessible and where the foe will be far removed from his own base and cut off from all succor in case of reverse, nothing is needed to render our triumph certain, but the exhi-bition of our own unquenchable resolve. Let us but will it, and we are free, and who, in the light of the past dare doubt your purpose in the future. Antimated by that confidence in your spirit and fortitude which never yet has failed me, I announce to you, fellow countrymen, that it is my purpose to maintain your cause with my whole heart and soul; that I will never consent to abandon to the enemy one foot of the soil of any of the States of the Confederacy . . . If by stress of numbers we should be compelled to a temporary withdrawal from [Virginia's] limits or those of any other border state, again and again we will return, until the baffled exhausted enemy shall abandon in despair his endless and impossible task of making slaves of people resolved to be free. Let us not then despond, my countrymen, but relying on the never failing mercies and protecting care of our God, let us meet the foe with fresh devi-ance, with unconquerable hearts.

It was an unbelievable statement. The whole concept of the Confederacy was a fight for what it saw as decency, for home and family. Here was President Jefferson Davis calling on the troops to enter a new phase of war; to become roving bands at-tacking the enemy and then retreating to hide. Many fights for freedom began as guerrilla operations and turned into legitimate government, but Davis proposed to turn a legitimate govern-ment into a guerrilla band.

In any event it mattered little, for only a handful of Confederates ever read the message before its content became moot. The Danville paper published it but few other journals received it in time. Finishing his message, Davis probably called on his cabinet ministers to see how their arrangements were coming and continued to make inquiries after Lee.

4. Money Exchange

In another part of town, on siding number two, between Craghead Street and Linn Street, the clerks of the treasury office set up a table beside the engine of the treasure train for the exchange of Confederate money into U.S. silver specie.

Walter Philbrook wrote, "At Danville, some of the specie was paid out under informal requisitions, the Secretary, Mr. Trenholm, and Mr. Hendren, the Treasurer, both being absent I think." He further mentioned that the requisitions that he subsequently honored were signed by Mr. Nutt.

Executive clerk, Micajah H. Clark, confirmed that he knew this exchange of silver for currency had occurred just as it had in Richmond a couple of days earlier. The rate of inflation had grown from 60-to-1 to 70-to-1 in the short span of 2 days.

The citizens of Danville and Pittsylvania County, already suffering from deprivation and loss during the four years of conflict, had little remaining extra money. Their reluctance to participate in the exchange program was understandable when considering that seventy paper dollars would only buy one silver dollar.

C. April 5, 1865

1. Waiting For Lee

Davis still had heard nothing from General Lee and the anxiety began to tell on him. Since Breckinridge had not come, he continued trying to run the war, but the efforts were mere form and meaningless.

Telegraphing in obvious displeasure over the removal of a subordinate in command of a small district, he actually snapped at his brother-in-law Richard Taylor in Mississippi. Davis ordered a replacement and advised Taylor that the new man "will not be removed without authority."

He also tried to coordinate General Cobb with others in Georgia and Alabama for the defense of southwestern Georgia and even ordered Beauregard to come to Danville to superintend the laying out of its new defenses.

Many of Semme's men were not needed on the fortifications and they gathered at the newly established Naval Store to write letters while others fished in the Dan River.

These were hectic but pleasant hours for Davis' staff. "We had a good time at Danville," Preston Johnston thought. Sharing the Sutherlins' hospitality proved to be very comfortable. A host of assorted officers came through the town, the flotsam of the collapsing war in Virginia. Troublesome Humphrey Marshall of Kentucky saw Davis briefly, and the President met others as he frequently rode around Danville's defenses, repeatedly commenting on their poor layout.

While most of the Confederate officials considered this a time of respite, it was entirely different for the Secretary of the Treasury. Trenholm's concerns were not only for his waning health but more so for the treasure for which he had complete responsibility. Accumulating money had been the focus of his attention during his entire life. Now he felt the awesome responsibility of managing the useful resources in the Confederate treasure while preventing the dreaded Federals from gaining any benefit from the rest of it. Whatever his thoughts were on the subject was never publicly disclosed. However, it can be surmised from his actions that he was in constant discussion regarding this matter with William D. Nutt, in whom he had gained confidence and trust.

President Davis' mind was also in turmoil. "Throughout that day Davis fidgeted at the lack of news from Lee." All he heard was Danville telegrapher Tredway's report that the Army of Northern Virginia was believed to be fighting somewhere near Amelia Court House.

2. Battlefield Reports

Daily, scores of wounded and disillusioned rebel soldiers lounged on the raised platform of the train depot. They dangled their legs from the splintered wooden floor and traded wild stories of real or imagined bravado, eventually admitting to losing one skirmish after another. The stragglers, amidst scads of macho tales, also sadly reported that supplies of food and munitions did not arrive at the battlefields as expected.

As news of these failing conditions persisted, the President discussed the continuing reports of frustration and deterioration with Secretary Trenholm and Secretary Mallory.

If those dire stories weren't enough to depress the most ebullient spirit, Jefferson Davis and the cabinet members were apprised of another situation that existed within the thickly constructed walls of the Sutherlin house where most of the Confederate officials had established residence.

No doubt, President Davis' three aides, Lubbock, Wood and Johnston inquired about how much privacy and secretiveness could the Cabinet expect at their meetings. Mr. Sutherlin casually replied that there was a Yankee in the house but there was no need to fret. Venerable Levi Holbrook, Sr. was 75 years old, too feeble to perform acts of treason against the Confederate government and, in his humble opinion, too honorable to have the desire.

3. Yankee In The House

Lubbock, Johnston and John Taylor Wood, members of the President's personal staff were the first to inquire about the quiet old man living on the first floor. By April 7, Secretaries Mallory and Trenholm became apprised of this mysterious man, also.

All that was revealed was that Levi Holbrook was a bachelor, one of Danville's first school teachers, the headmaster of the Danville Male Academy and that he was notoriously private.

Strange that he preferred to be solitude, but he did. Sought-after privacy, like planned parenthood, breeds its own kind in its own time. The New England reserve, the seldom shown emotion, the calculating nature, the remoteness of control, the deliberate distance, all bred the same loneliness and neglect he sired.

Most of all, he was an enigma. The puzzle included pieces that didn't fit. During the War between the States, and after, whispers whizzed about him. "He was wealthy but lost it all." "He's a confirmed bachelor." "He has no family." He did nothing to dispel the rumors nor deny their disturbing inconsistencies.

A self-constructed shell isolated him from society and seemed impenetrable. However, a minute crack in the crust permitted a sliver of light into his charcoal world. One of his peers, Dr. George Washington Dame, created the crevice when he chronicled, "He had a son living in New York in 1895." It blew his cover. Questions began to surface. A bachelor with a son in New York. Was he an unwed father? Were there other unfounded tales, other contradictions?

Ten years of dogged detective work wedged into the doubt, into the life that resisted research for over a century.

Levi Holbrook. Undeniably the most interesting person to ever live in Danville was also the most intriguing. Possessed with a penchant for privacy, his life was one that confounded contemporaries and confused historians. The mystery surrounding his person was one that he orchestrated. Only recently has the mask been lifted to reveal the real Levi.

He was born June 10, 1789 in Holden, a quiet village in northern Massachusetts. The farm family had fourteen children, all with Biblical names, typically expanded by the need of many hands to till the soil. This attachment to the earth didn't prevent his mother, Patience, from insisting that all her children learn to read. After reading his first book and random issues of Worcester newspapers, Levi was never the same. The bizarre teenager had no interest in dirt nor in farm animals. Other family members might cultivate the soil; he would cultivate the classics.

At age nineteen, he could think of nothing but a formal education and in 1808, enrolled in the University of Vermont. It was the one place he could pursue his own form of escapism. After graduation in 1811, any help he offered at the farm was halfhearted at best, despite parental pressures that implored him to stay home and help with myriad agricultural chores. Only Micah, a brother, understood his need for individuality and independence.

Rather than submit to what he believed a dismal life of drudgery he planned a real escape. Detection was difficult the night he secreted out, dressed in a favorite short Eton jacket, and headed south – away from the earth that bored him; away from menial tasks that stifled him. Levi hoped to utilize the teaching skills learned in Vermont.

In the early 1800s, teachers with credentials in North Carolina, as in all of the South, were a much-sought-after commodity. Arriving in Caswell County, North Carolina in 1812, University of Vermont diploma protruding from a pocket, there was an immediate welcome and the offer of the headmaster's job at Hico Academy. This short man with boney fingers held a university diploma, a carriage that made him seem bigger than his meager frame and a demeanor that made him seem aloof. To the untrained eye, they were all qualities needed to produce a professor.

Although not a warm person, he was obviously capable. Testimony to unbelievable proficiency, which included a healthy knowledge of the classics and a hefty dose of seriousness, was the honorary master's degree awarded by the University of North Carolina. What an incredible achievement! – recognition the first year on the job! Echoing two years later, the Doctor of Divinity degree was conferred by the same university, given "for distinguishing himself by excellence in teaching."

The art of teaching was a pioneer profession. It was difficult to evaluate something so incredibly novel. A very good teacher presumably could charge phenomenal prices for the craft and get away with it. Teaching, in the formative years, became a lucrative occupation, as evidenced by the premium attached to it. No matter that he charged $300 to $500 per student per annum. Word spread rapidly of his ability and subsequent recognition.

Wealthy Danville families, notably the Wilson's, heard these stories. In 1804, they had encouraged the building of the Danville Male Academy, a rough-hewn log school, centrally located in a grove of locust trees. The first educators knew the effectiveness of discipline (Ox sticks were used to tame recalcitrant students.), but there was not an equal measure of learning to balance the books. Everyone expressed hope that Levi could be lured to Danville.

Invited, he decided to come to Danville to become the headmaster of the Academy. The catalyst was cash. Three years at Hico Academy enabled Levi to amass an enviable collection of books and a sizable sum of money.

When it was discovered that he had a wish to become an investor, he was convinced to buy in 1815 several acres of downtown Danville. By early 1816, he owned all of Craghead Street, Linn Street and Patton Street, half of the town. Over the years, this plat was divided and sold in profitable parcels to tobacco companies, businesses, residences and municipal government. These land deals, coupled with additional yearly student stipends, further fattened his fortune. Yet, he continued to give top priority to the educating of young men.

A typical day under his tutelage was marked by students sitting on their benches, as though at attention. A finger jabbed at a student meant he must recite from a book loaned overnight. Each book on loan had a printed bookmark . . .

> *Levi Holbrook. His good booke,*
> *God give him grace therein to looke,*
> *And whosoever steals this booke,*
> *He shall be hanged on a hooke,*
> *As high as ever one can looke.*

Demanding perfection, Levi required the pupil to recite from memory. Writing had to be equally exact, an uncrossed "t" or an undotted "i" bringing sure wrath and a possible flogging. Many students swore vengeance but never lived up to their vows.

In the off seasons, away from the classroom, he occasionally visited Massachusetts, re-establishing ties with the family he had abandoned several years earlier and seeking more investment opportunities. Evidence of financial success, marked by substantial purchases of Massachusetts bank stocks, was all it took to make them forget his past impertinence.

Levi wore his wealth well. He didn't flaunt it. Never decked out in sartorial splendor, his attire, marked by frayed sleeves and fading, would make one surmise that only a thread separated him from poverty. Observing his propensity for look-ing destitute, a family member flippantly commented, "You've made a great deal of money. Now you should enjoy it." His reply was both automatic and terse. "The only pleasure money gives me is in the making of more."

A new challenge came in 1826 when he became head-master of the new Female Academy. A teacher, Eliza Grout of Northborough, Massachusetts became his wife April 6, 1827. Afterwards, he built a substantial two-story house at the corner of Main and Craghead Streets. In 1828 an unexplained illness confined him to Holbrook House. While he was absent from school, Eliza became headmistress for six years. Regaining his health to return to work in 1834, he also sired a son, born March 6, 1836.

Three years later, Eliza died in Danville, tuberculosis be-ing the culprit. It was necessary to leave Danville temporarily to find a proper home for the toddler Levi, Jr. Like most loving mothers and doting grandmothers, Patience agreed to raise little Levi, but his sensible sibling, Micah, was entrusted with the funds to care for his upbringing and schooling.

During the decade 1840-1850 he returned to the field of education . . . the Danville Female Academy. Eighteen-fifty was the final year of a sparkling career of teaching. Until then, in-struction and investments shared equal billing. At age 61 he relinquished teaching to concentrate on economic issues, mak-ing an office in his home.

A spectacular fire in 1855 at the foot of Main Street de-stroyed seventeen businesses and Holbrook House. Looking at the smoldering ashes, remnants of the residence, Levi realized the utter futility of the bucket brigade. They had done nothing more than dampen the enthusiasm of the relentless flames. Danville had no real Fire Department. Thinking about the trag-edy made him do something totally out of character; he gave something away. It cost him $500.00 to buy Danville its first fire engine.

Dislocated by the disaster, he lived in different and un-satisfactory quarters for the next two years. Still owner of sev-eral pieces of desirable real estate, Levi had no enthusiasm to rebuild. A friend requested to buy a specific site on which to build a mansion. Levi agreed to sell the land to W. T. Sutherlin in 1857 provided he would have rent-free living space in the mansion for the rest of his life. As stipulated in the bargain, the completed grand house had a room with a private entrance for Mr. Holbrook.

The 1860 census stated that Levi Holbrook had $281,200 in the bank. Several times that year, Levi boarded the "train" (stage coach) for New York, large quantities of money in leather satchels also making the trip. Intimidated by his aloofness, no one queried him about the steady withdrawals nor the ultimate destination of the investments. Secretly, he had been buying original stock in the Bank of America. Still there were questions. Had he become senile at sixty years of age? Why would he take from "safe" depositories and transfer to unsure places? Why the regular removals? Was he involved in chasing financial folly? No one dared quiz him about it. If there were monetary miscues, it would be embarrassing to remind him of the mistakes, if he were wise, then equally embarrassing to be thought nosey. The safe stance was silence. Uncertain, questions converted to reality. Rumors circulated that he had been a poor entrepreneur and had lost everything. His contemporaries never realized that he had made a thoughtful and timely move.

When the Civil War broke out, he lived miserly, worn clothing and a stingy lifestyle underscoring the universal view of abject poverty. During the War, the 63-year-old visited Danville's six prisons daily, wondering if his son were among the captives. While there is no evidence that he opposed the war, one letter to his son did record some ambivalence to it, although he didn't support splitting up the Union to make another country.

There are also no indications that he associated with Jefferson Davis President of the Confederate States of America. Although they shared the same roof during the dying days of the Confederacy, there is no mention of a mere handshake. It is likely, by this time, that his shell of silence and solitude was too solidly formed.

Did the presence of a Yankee in the house disturb the President or members of the inner circle? Was something untoward said? Was there an unrecorded incident? Could that or some related thing have compelled a member of the inner circle to hide or bury a portion of the treasure in Danville?

It could be. Something did. We may never know the full story.

[In 1868 the 79-year-old departed the Sutherlin household and moved to 770 Main Street to live with the John Noble
Wyllie family until his death May 20, 1872.

He fooled everybody. They thought he died destitute
when, in fact he was worth millions. They thought he had no
family, but he had a formidable one.

His life was a puzzle. But as each discovery was made,
an interlocking piece of the jigsaw confirmed itself and gave credence to the next one.

When I first visited the Last Capital of the Confederacy
and the Sutherlin Mansion (Museum of Fine Arts and History),
the docent (guide) said, "Levi Holbrook was a bachelor." Everyone was deluded. The bachelor was married.]

4. Secretaries Confer

The treasure train's tent encampment was not a happy
place. Bank and treasury clerks were influenced by less-than-
dedicated wives and by other clerks, whose shaky stability fluc-
tuated between jubilation at having escaped capture and ner-
vous breakdown worrying about the future. Lieutenant W. H.
Parker noted that Senior Teller Walter Philbrook had become
somewhat entangled in that web in instability.

He wrote, "This was a source of annoyance to me from
that time forward because I thought it was a time when every
man should be made to do his duty."

On one of his visits to the guards' encampment on Linn
Street, Secretary Mallory tried to relax on the top of a box inside
Parker's tent while he conferred confidentially with him. Lieutenant Parker was frank when he requested Mr. Mallory to see
the Secretary of the Treasury regarding the Confederate Treasurer and Assistant Treasurer accompanying the treasure. "It
was their duty to be with it at this time. I did not think it right
that it should be left with a teller as the senior civil officer."

5. The Inner Circle

Because telegraph lines had been severed by marauding
Federal troops, very few messages arrived at the depot of the

Danville and Midland Railroad on Craghead Street. Those few that made it were deciphered by telegrapher Tredway and relayed by messengers on horseback to the Confederate Offices.

Every bleak report was soberly pondered by clerks entrusted with that duty, filtered for what demanded the most attention and then forwarded to the appropriate Cabinet department post to deal with as they saw fit. Little but disastrous messages came across their desks. Disappointed clerks found it difficult to read those glum reports and even more humiliating to decide their relative importance. Some of the messages required the President's personal attention and others, of lesser importance, could be handled by his subordinates.

Cabinet officers read these briefs, compiled the telegraphed data and prepared written summaries for the daily Cabinet meetings. Many of these meetings were held at the Sutherlin Mansion due to Jefferson Davis' desire to have all cabinet members attend the meetings. Trenholm could not make it to the Confederate Office on Wilson Street so Davis accommodated his needs.

Some messages were of such a critical nature, requiring an immediate decision and prompt action, that Jefferson Davis unilaterally called upon the wisdom of the Secretary of the Navy, Stephen Mallory and the very ill Secretary of the Treasury, George Trenholm to assist him in making expeditious but sane decisions. While in Danville, these three, all residing in the same household, in effect, became the inner circle.

D. April 6, 1865

1. Little To Do

There was little for Davis or the Cabinet to do in Danville. In this vacuum some Confederate leaders began to dream that perhaps Lee had scored a military victory over Grant and the Union Army was on the defensive. Mallory later wrote, "To a few, very few, they were days of hope; to the many, they were days of despondency, if not despair; and to all, days of intense anxiety." Haw, of the Ordnance Department, called the week "a season of suspense."

There was little to do for most of the cabinet members. Judah Benjamin spent long hours discussing his favorite poet Tennyson with his roommate Hoge.

2. The Sutherlin's Concern

The President's hostess grew more concerned as she watched him day after day. He was uniformly "pleasant and agreeable and self-possessed," she thought, "but he would not eat or partook but little while his aides ravenously consumed her cooking." His only solace seemed to come from listening to that mockingbird who presented early morning concerts and from afternoon conversations with Major Sutherlin in his library. Davis' mood swung rapidly from optimism to resignation, then back again, and from the present to the past. He spoke of his love of farming, recalled fondly his Mexican War days, then recounted the fall of Richmond, at the same time expressing his unshakable confidence in Lee. "I think under all the circumstances we have done the best we could," the President went on. He spoke of the resources against them and rehearsed his old inner debate about taking young boys into the armies to fight, "grinding seed-corn" as he called it. One evening, while sitting up late smoking cigars under the trees in front of the Major's house, Sutherlin cautioned Davis to look to his own safety. Grant was before him and Sherman at his rear. "Do not delay so in your journey," said Sutherlin. "Let your movements be as rapid and veiled as possible."

3. Sayler's Creek

April 6th dealt a tragic blow to the 18th Virginia Infantry. Danville's contingency, Companies A and B, felt the sting of defeat at Saylers's Creek as thirty-two of Danville's men fought there.

Second Lieutenant John H. Holland of Company A jumped in front of his Danville Blues, waved his sword and yelled, "Follow me boys!" The entire left of the Confederate line surged forward in attack as screams of the *Rebel Yell* echoed over the din of musketry. Within minutes, hand-to-hand fighting had erupted in fields and amid wet woods. The bravery of 2nd Lieutenant Holland resulted in a gunshot wound to his right leg. Lieutenant Robert S. Jones from Company A also received life-threatening wounds in that skirmish. All members of the Danville Blues were captured. Twelve of them were taken to Point Lookout Prison, where they lived miserably for more than two grueling months. One of the incarcerated, William A. Baily, died there as a result of chronic diarrhea.

Below is a list of those Confederate soldiers from the Danville Blues who were marched away to Point Lookout Prison.

Baily, William A.
Baptist, Nathaniel W.
Brazzlia, Lewis
Buford, William Henry
Dunkley, William F.
Hall, James M.
Harvey, William H.
Price, Joel M.
Shields, David T.
Walters, Robert Alexander
Wilson, Nathaniel

Danville sent eighteen men of Company B into this battle. In late afternoon, superior numbers of Federal troops bored in on their position. Realizing the futility of continuing the fight, all eighteen of them dropped their weapons, raised their hands and were marched off to Point Lookout Prison. All except one, John Chocklett, survived the more than two months of confinement. He developed a bad case of measles and died there before he could gain his freedom.

Danville Grays (Company B) who were imprisoned at Point Lookout include the following:

Abell, Benjamin F.
Barnes, James Allen
Chambers, Armistead B.
Chocklett, John
Cunningham, John T.
Davis, James E.

Flippen, Robert M.
Jordan, S. H.
Kemp, Peter A.
Moore, William J.
Neal, James Mastin
Payne, William Fleming
Pigg, Hezekiah
Richardson, Eugene A.
Robinson, Edward D.
Singleton, William B.
Thompson, William B.
Wilkerson, Stephen A.

Danville had suffered much at the battle of Saylers' Creek, the most important of those last struggles of which Grant said, "There was as much gallantry displayed by some of the Confederates in these little engagements as was displayed at any time during the war, notwithstanding the sad defeats of the past weeks."

Even those hardened by the war shed tears over bad news so close to home, especially when the next day two beaten and wounded men came back home with news that thirty of Danville's brave men had been captured and were being marched off to prison.

4. Moving Again

Thursday morning came with no new information from Lee. Uneasy because of this, the inner circle met and decided to activate their contingency plans regarding the treasure.

Since Davis was concerned with another matter of government, establishing an executive office in Danville, he called upon Mallory and Trenholm to put the contingency plans into action. Trenholm issued orders to Lt. Parker to convey the remaining treasure further south to Charlotte, North Carolina for safety and then await further orders.

Parker called a meeting of his middies at the front of the tent encampment. He told them to take down the tents, pack all of their paraphernalia and prepare to move south.

Parker had earlier requested someone other than Philbrook be in charge of the treasure, especially mentioning John Hendren, the Treasurer, or the Assistant Treasurer, as his replacement. Secretary Mallory consulted with fellow cabinet member and friend Secretary Trenholm to have President Davis write an order for John Hendren to accompany the treasure train to Greensboro and wait there for further orders from the Secretary of the Treasury.

Since Secretary Trenholm had first-hand knowledge of Hendren's lack of maturity and dependability, he sought permission from President Davis to have the executive clerk, M. H. Clark take charge of the Confederate treasure.

President Davis granted Trenholm's request.

Eager to accept this new responsibility, Clark packed his carpetbag and rode a buggy to the treasure train on Linn Street. When he arrived, there was no time to make a complete accounting of the specie in the treasure. Clark presented his written orders from Secretary Trenholm to William Philbrook and established his unilateral control over the treasure.

Another order was quietly delivered to the chief clerk of the Treasury, William D. Nutt. That order from Secretary Trenholm required the chief clerk to remain in Danville and move his sleeping quarters to the Confederate Offices on Wilson Street while the treasure train moved south. Thinking he may never see them again, Major Nutt said a tearful good-bye to his daughter and son-in-law, Peter Wise, and moved his belongings to the new quarters.

As soon as the gold was returned to the treasure train from the Bank of Danville, it was placed with the rest of the Confederate treasure already on board. Hurriedly, the clerks and their wives brought their personal effects onto the train and took their respective places on one of the rail cars. Last to board the train were the guards who had assumed protection of the treasure until all the gold was in place.

It was late evening when the treasure train backed out of siding two. The rear of the train was on the trestle bridge when the engine was shifted to the forward gears and redirected onto the main narrow gauge track where it proceeded slowly south to Greensboro.

Meanwhile, back at the Sutherlin Mansion, President Davis sat in front of the desk with pen in hand to write Varina. He chose his words carefully not wishing to upset her about the current uncertain condition of the government, "We are now fixing an executive office where the current business may be transacted here."

E. April 7, 1865

Union soldiers had defeated the Danville Blues (Company A) at Sayler's Creek on April 6 despite the notable bravery shown by its men who in the face of unbelievable adversity charged straight into enemy lines led by 2nd Lieutenant John H. Holland. He and another Lieutenant, Robert S. Jones, showed gallantry in the midst of obvious defeat and both were wounded. The wounds sustained by Lieutenant Jones were of such a serious nature that he was close to death.

Although the Federals captured the entire Company they were left with a quandary. They wanted to march the captured soldiers to Point Lookout Prison. However, marching was impossible for two non-ambulatory soldiers, Lieutenants Holland and Jones. Why wasn't captured soldier Augustus W. Garrett marched off to prison with the others? Could it be that the Union captors were faced with a problem of two wounded rebels? In order to resolve that problem, a decision was made to permit the healthiest captured soldier, six-foot-two inch Augustus to return to Danville with his wounded comrades.

That is how three men from Company A returned to Danville (probably in a wagon) in the pre-dawn hours of April 8, 1865.

F. April 8, 1865

1. Sutherlin Mansion

From his headquarters in the mansion, Davis continued trying to perform the routine duties of his office the next day, making appointments, looking after railroad communications and receiving news from the three Sayler's Creek survivors who had returned to Danville.

George Moore Livery Stable;
Horses & Wagon Borrowed to Transport Treasure to Burial site

When a report arrived that Yankee cavalry were believed to be coming toward Danville from the west, reserves quickly went out. Some went to the breastworks, designed to protect Danville from Federal troops from the northeast, while another contingency of troops headed to the northwest.

Burton Harrison, Davis' personal aide who had accompanied Varina Davis and children to Charlotte, arrived in the early evening of the 8th. He found the government in a turbulent uproar all the time "with a host of matters to attend to." Still, he wrote, "as nothing like sounds of battle could be heard in the country round about, we inferred that the situation had been improved."

The Sutherlin Mansion returned to relative calm.

2. The Wise Report

It was about eight o'clock in the evening of that Saturday when the hoofs of Lieutenant Wise' horse resounded on the bridge which spanned the Dan River at Danville. When Wise arrived, the lights of Danville were a welcome sight. The town was crowded with people, the result of the recent influx from Richmond. At the Exchange Hotel, he learned that President Davis was domiciled at the home of Major Sutherlin and he continued on to his destination.

A sentry at the yard gate challenged him. He announced his name, rank, mission and was admitted. In a few moments Burton Harrison appeared saying the President and his Cabinet were meeting in the dining-room and requested his report. He was the first person to bring direct news from General Lee.

At the meeting were the President, Burton Harrison, Mr. Benjamin, General Breckinridge, Secretary Mallory, Secretary Reagan, and several others who sat around a large dining-table asking a number of questions. He was intimidated by the group but Mr. Davis soon put him at ease.

3. Hidden Liability

Having recently heard the depressing news delivered by Lieutenant Wise, Secretary Trenholm sent his clerk, John Ott to the Confederate Offices on Wilson Street. Courier Ott delivered urgent orders to summon Chief Clerk William Deakins Nutt to his bedside. Realizing the import of the message, the chief clerk and Secretary Ott hurried to the Sutherlin Mansion.

When they arrived at Secretary Trenholm's sick room, Major Nutt listened to the sad news about the potential fall of the government. Believing that the Confederate treasure in Danville may be in imminent danger of being captured by the Union troops, Secretary Trenholm explained that the Mexican coins (forty-nine unopened kegs) still in the Treasury Office on Wilson Street, had to be concealed. Because the Mexican silver dollars weighed nearly 10,000 pounds, continuing to travel with such a cumbersome load would have required at least four two-horse wagons. Having to travel slowly, Trenholm surmised, the Federals would surely capture the wagons and confiscate the specie for themselves.

Major Nutt agreed and asked what he could do to help. Secretary Trenholm replied that the Mexican silver dollars were of no immediate use to the government because foreign currency could not be spent readily. In other words, what had originally been an asset, had become a liability. Although the Mexican silver dollars could not benefit the Confederate government, he certainly did not want the Federal forces to rejoice in capturing such a large amount of specie. The trio decided that the best thing to do was to bury surreptitiously all 49 kegs. Trenholm asked Secretary Ott and Major Nutt to swear on their honor that they would never reveal to anyone where the kegs of Mexican silver dollars would be buried.

In a letter to R. A. Lancaster written October 23, 1865, Major Nutt proved the sincerity of his commitment which he kept until his death. "In whatever business of locality circumstances may place me, be assured that next to the proper discharge of **a trust confided to my honor**, an opportunity to promote your interest or pleasure, will be most agreeable to me, and command properly my best energies."

Having sworn to honor the integrity of the Confederate States of America, that they would never divulge the trust placed in them, the two treasury employees left the bedside of the Secretary, calculating how they would fulfill the special written orders that had been presented to them. The orders read simply: "Release all the specie to the care of Major Nutt and John Ott." Signed G. A. Trenholm, Secretary of the Treasury.

Major Nutt made an agreement with John Ott to take this order to the Confederate Offices so that the treasury clerks would release the Mexican silver dollars into their care. After taking possession of the kegs, Ott would wait for him there.

The chief clerk went straight down Main Street hill and turned left to the livery stable owned by George Moore. Upon arriving, he requested, once more, to borrow that same sturdy wagon and the two fine draught horses for another project. Again, Moses Davis hitched Isaac and Jacob to the wagon and passed the reigns to Major Nutt.

In the darkness a short time elapsed before William Nutt drove the wagon to the white wooden gate in front of the Benedict House where John Ott waited. At that time they received help loading thirteen casks onto the wagon. A plank which sat on top of the drums would make it easy for them to roll the 195-pound kegs into their resting place. This was the first of four trips that was made to the burial site. Shovels full of yellow, loamy Piedmont soil covered the fortune with a blanket that has

not been moved nor shifted for 131 years.
Palm Sunday waited on the horizon.

G. April 9, 1865

Unity Service

Palm Sunday morning arrived without a cloud in the sky.
Could it be that the pleasant change in the weather could also signal the changing of fortunes for the South? From the Allen and Ayres residences located near the Episcopal Church, the fragrance of spring-time daffodils permeated the air. Pollock wrote, "The cessation of all traffic gave our place a Sabbath stillness."

Bells from the warehouse towers, the courthouse, and the belfries of four churches rang in unison, inviting local citizens to a joint service at the Episcopal Church of the Epiphany. Pollock put it this way, "This service was to be one emphasizing the determination of this town to remain unified in its dedication to the Southern cause."

The centrally-located Episcopal Church on the northeast corner of Jefferson Street and Main Street, was chosen to host the combined worship service. In expectation of many early worshippers, organist Mary Pace walked briskly from her home on Jefferson Street to the church. She felt keenly the importance of the prelude in establishing a positive mood for the unity service.

While the music played, multitudes of parishioners entered the sanctuary hoping to find a pew in close proximity to the rows reserved for the President, his Cabinet and assorted officials. Some prestigious local citizens were also afforded reserved seating including the Mayor, President and members of the Common Council and Major W. T. Sutherlin.

Those in attendance upon divine worship found the service to be one of ambivalence-gloom and glory.

The Episcopal rector, the Reverend George Washington Dame, quietly gave the sad details of the Sayler's Creek tragedy that had occurred three days earlier, read the names of those who had been imprisoned and lifted up prayers for them. Then

The Episcopal Church
Where President Davis worshipped Palm Sunday April 9, 1865
(Courtesy of The Episcopal Church of the Epiphany)

he told the local faithful that one of their flock, who lived with his merchant partner W. T. Clark, and who had been severely wounded in that same battle, had "taken a turn for the worse". More prayers were said for him.

The minister reminded the citizens that all was not lost, that in the midst of all this gloom, some good may yet come of it, that they should not give up hope.

After the benediction was read at the Unity church service, one of Danville's most respected citizens was quietly and solemnly laid to rest in a simple grave in Green Hill Cemetery.

One would surmise that since over two-hundred fighting young men of Danville during the Civil War were serving in the 18th Virginia or Cabell's Battery most of their graves would be easily identified. Though Green Hill Cemetery was purchased by the town in 1863, during the midst of the conflict, few markers can be found to indicate those who died during this period.

The grave of Episcopal parishioner, Robert S. Jones sits alone in the center of a family block normally reserved for a dozen graves. Strangely, no other tombstones occupy the space. According to official records of the Confederate Armies, the gunshot wounds received at Sayler's Creek on April 6 did not prove to be fatal until April 27, three weeks later. James I. Robertson wrote that he was buried in Green Hill Cemetery, Danville and "is probably the last war fatality in the 18th Virginia".

The almost illegible, speckled, gray headstone of Jones partially reads:

In Memory of

Lieut. R. S. Jones

Co. A 18th Va. Reg.

Died of wounds received

in the battle of Sailor's Creek

in the 28th year of his age

A gallant soldier

A Christian gentleman

He must have been a short man because the distance from the headstone to the footstone is barely five feet. On one half of the double footstone is inscribed CV1. Although small of stature, this soldier was large in reputation because the foot of his headstone pays him the ultimate tribute "Gallant soldier, Christian gentleman".

Many who fought at Sayler's Creek were Christian gentlemen, Dr. Dame preached. "But no matter what our fate," he went on, "to God be the glory!"

That afternoon Davis returned from church in good spirits.

Sunday night, Davis dined with Major and Mrs. Sutherlin still unaware that Lee had surrendered. At one point, Mrs. Sutherlin asked Davis if the war would be over should Lee surrender. "By no means," the President replied. "We'll fight it out to the Mississippi River."

It was a long time before Davis knew some of the details of that memorable Palm Sunday.

H. April 10, 1865

Monday morning dawned with heavy gray clouds in the sky and brought with it the first indications that the end was at hand. Semmes watched as scores of wounded soldiers returned from losses on the battlefields.

Early Monday afternoon Davis took a carriage to the Benedict House to confer with his fellow government officials. He had planned to stay at the house a short time, but rain began falling and quickly turned into a violent storm. He decided to remain for dinner and waited as the meal was prepared in what had been the kitchen for a girl's school.

At 3:30, Captain W. P. Graves, a messenger from Lee, arrived at the headquarters of General Harrison Walker who commanded some 3,000 troops in and around Danville. Harrison sent Graves to the Benedict House where Graves found Davis and handed him a brief note. Davis sat very still as he read it, then turned pale. The cabinet members scanned the message. They realized how important it was to take prompt action because in a short time they must prepare to move South.

Benjamin returned to the Grasty House to pack. There he found the Rev. Hoge talking with two women. He talked briefly with the three, then pulled Hoge aside saying, "I did not have the heart to tell those good ladies what I have just learned. General Lee has surrendered and I fear the Confederate cause is lost."

[The *Danville Register,* January 22, 1939 repeated what happened that day at the home of Colonel Grasty. Jennie Grasty, his daughter, talked about how everyone was saddened by the news. Within a short time they were preparing to leave. Miss Grasty took a cooked ham from the stove and gave it to the departing group "to sustain them on their travels."]

Davis returned to the Sutherlin house to prepare for the move to Greensboro. Virginia Governor William "Extra Billy" Smith arrived at the house late Monday and learned of Lee's retreat for the first time from Davis who said, "Well sir, though unofficial, I have no doubt of the fact. You see my people packing up and I shall be off as soon as possible."

The Old Grasty House, Built 1810, Danville, Virginia.
(*Courtesy of Lawrence McFall*)

Since Governor Smith of Virginia had also fled south to Danville in the crisis following the fall of Richmond, establishing headquarters first at the home of Witcher Keen, Esq., and then at the residence of Captain W. T. Clark on the corner of Main and South Ridge Streets, the little town was doubly, if briefly, a capital city, both of the Confederate States and of the State of Virginia.; Honors "that came without seeking and passed away without regret." (Pollock)

The people of Danville had clearly enjoyed the short-lived honor of being the capital of the Confederacy. They knew what had happened to Richmond just one week before and now feared that their city would be next.

Following the overwhelming news of General Lee's surrender came reports of an advancing force of the Federal army, agitated citizens behaved foolishly. Miss Clara Read buried her silver so hurriedly and securely that she could never remember the spot. It was never found, though the small boys of succeeding years "instead of going out hunting for pirate gold, went looking for Miss Clara's silver." Somewhere on Green Street it probably lies buried today.

Hallowed memories and deeply rooted sentiment have grown up around that tragic week. Hospitable homes had thrown open their doors to the distinguished visitors and their attendant officials and scarcely a home was without one or more guests.

Before Davis would leave, he insisted on writing letters of appreciation to the mayor and city council of Danville. He wrote Mayor J. M. Walker thanking him for the generous reception of himself and his executive officers. "The shadows of misfortune which were on us when I came have become darker, and I trust you accord to me now, as then, your good wishes and confidence."

He wired to Beauregard to disregard his earlier instructions to come to Danville and instead to join Johnston in North Carolina.

As preparations for leaving Danville approached completion. Jefferson Davis' iron self-control won out again, and Preston Johnston found him "as collected as ever."

That evening he returned to the Sutherlin house and personally broke the news to his hostess, almost whispering that he must leave Danville as quickly as possible. After packing he gave her a pen as a memento. The Sutherlins begged him to take a thousand dollars in gold they had hoarded for some time, but Davis only broke into tears at their generosity. "I cannot," he protested. "God bless you and yours." He stepped into his carriage at 9:30 and left for the depot.

At ten o'clock government officals gathered near the cars sitting on their luggage "in a little silent group by themselves in the darkness, lighted only by Mr. Benjamin's inextinguishable cigar." Multitudes of frightened people were trying to board the Davis' train.

A few men were hoping to join Johnston's army to continue the fight; others were seeking to get out of Danville by any means. Davis and anyone who looked like a government official was surrounded by anxious citizens and soldiers seeking a seat.

Mallory later wrote that nothing seemed to be in order. The Presidential train did not leave until nearly eleven o'clock. The depot could only be reached through knee deep mud. In the darkness, the crowds were yelling and cursing, determined to board in defiance of the guards.

Colonel Burton Harrison was put in charge of the evacuation, but he was no match for the job. He was approached by a general from the torpedo department with his two daughters in tow. The general sought seats for himself and his family and freight space for some of his explosives. Harrison said no, but the general, an old friend, obtained permission to board from President Davis.

One of the daughters of the general from the torpedo bureau sat down next to Davis and began chatting. Davis sat motionless while she talked about the weather and her dresses and shot dozens of questions at Davis. Her voice could be heard throughout the car, since she was the only one talking.

In the midst of her chattering, there was a sharp explosion near Davis, and everyone in the car quickly jumped fearing the worst. A young man, assigned to the general from the torpedo bureau grabbed the seat of his pants with both hands. It turned out he had an explosive device in his pocket that went off when he sat on a stove in the car.

The ten original cars were so overcrowded that two additional cars had to be added over the protests of the trainmen. The train lurched forward, then stopped. Again, it lurched forward and this time traveled nearly five miles before coming to a stop. [Probably where the Danville Golf Club is today.] The weight of the cars was too much for the engine and a cylinder had broken. Another engine was quickly brought up and the train moved on. This was around midnight.

Back in Danville, two companies of soldiers had been left behind to protect the food and ammunition left by the government. No sooner had the Davis train departed than a rowdy crowd began to gather at the storehouse. Finally, a woman yelled, "Our children and we'uns are starving; the Confederacy is gone up; let us help ourselves." The guards were pushed away and the storehouses looted. In the midst of the looting a nearby ammunition train exploded, killing fifty civilians and soldiers.

In the fear and confusion, no one noticed, even cared, that forty-nine kegs from the Treasury Office had been left behind.

THE REPORTS

A. Greensboro - The Interim Report

In Danville on the 6th of April, President Davis had written a special order for Hendren to be read in Greensboro.

Mr. Hendren: C. S. Treasurer, Greensboro, North Carolina

Sir: You will report to General Beauregard with the treasure in your possession, that he may give to it due protection as a military chest to be moved with his army train. For further instructions you will report to the Secretary of the Treasury.

Jefferson Davis.
Official: F. R. Lubbock, Colonel and A. D. C.

On April 6th the Confederate treasure train pulled into the depot at Greensboro. The specie that started out from Richmond was valued at around $523,000 and weighed over 22,000 pounds, 7,000 pounds more than the freight car was designed to carry.

By the time the treasure reached Greensboro, it had been reduced by $196,000 and 9,555 pounds (the value and the weight of forty-nine kegs of Mexican silver dollars).

Capt. Micajah H. Clark left his position as executive clerk in Danville to take charge of the C.S.A. treasure. He reported the treasure was $327,022.90 when it arrived in Greensboro. He calculated this amount by the fact that $39,000 in silver had been left under charge of the Treasurer, Mr. John C. Hendren to be paid to General Johnston's troops as a military chest. At that time the amount of specie remaining in the Treasure was $288,022.90.

John Hendren
(The Library of Virginia)

The silver specie left with Treasurer Hendren was a melange of several different silver coins, $35,000 in U.S. silver and the one opened cask of Mexican silver dollars (8 Reales pieces).

Lieutenant Wise wrote that Hendren paid General Johnston's troops and each received $1.15 in silver. Some of the dollars were U.S. silver dollars but 4,000 of them were the Mexican silver dollars bearing the Mint Mark O. He received his dollar (a Mexican silver dollar) at "Jimtown" [Jamestown, North Carolina] where he was paroled. Wise had intended to scratch his initials in his Mexican silver dollar but awoke the next morning to find that it had been stolen. He reported that Johnston's soldiers, upon receiving their silver, sang a little diddy, "one dollar and fifteen cents for four years work."

[Three Mexican silver dollars have surfaced. Two of them can be seen on display at the Museum of the Confederacy in Richmond, Virginia.]

Before leaving for Charlotte with the treasure train, M. H. Clark left two boxes of gold sovereigns, valued at $35,000, with the Confederate officials "for the use of Davis and the Cabinet".

At this time the majority of the specie became separated from the President, the Cabinet and other government officials. It continued on to Charlotte, N. C. by train, its contents under direct supervision of M H. Clark and still watched over by William H. Parker and the sixty guards. Subtracting the $35,000 in gold sovereigns he had left with officials in Greensboro, the balance of the Confederate treasure leaving for Charlotte was $253,022.90. The overall weight of the Confederate treasure had again been reduced by more than 2,000 pounds (around 2,298 pounds of silver and 129 pounds of gold).

Walter Philbrook's letter to the *New York Times* reported, "It seems that the President would not take a dollar for his personal use and I do not know that any of his immediate party received a share of it." The high civil officers and the military commanders intended to make this money go as far as possible in enabling the soldiers to reach their homes without sufferings, and without causing distress to others.

The interim report in Greensboro of the accounting of funds in the Confederate treasure might have been adequate documentation to show there is *Confederate Treasure in Danville.*

However, M. H. Clark's report of the final disposition of funds in the Confederate treasure certainly substantiates it.

B. M. H. Clark - The Final Report

The most authentic report came from the "clear and conclusive statement by the last Acting Treasurer of the Confederacy, Captain M. H. Clark" submitted to the Editor of the *Courier-Journal* in Clarksville, Tennessee and published January 10, 1882. It was the purpose of his compilation that it would be a full statement of the final disposition of the Confederate specie at the close of the war "which shall forever set at rest the miserable slanders against President Davis, which have so often been refuted only to be revived by the malignity of his enemies."

COL. MICAJAH HENRY CLARK
Tobacconist
Ex. Chief and Con. Clerk Executive Office C. S. A.
and Ex. Acting Treas. C. S. A.
Clarksville

Micajah Henry Clark
(The Library of Virginia)

Micajah Henry Clark stated to the newspaper how he came to be the last Acting Treasurer of the Confederacy and presented a brief synopsis of the route the treasure took from Richmond, Virginia to Washington, Georgia. His report also specified to whom distributions were made and detailed how much of the treasure was paid out at each location.

Clark was the chief and confidential clerk of the Executive office when Richmond, Virginia had to be evacuated the night of April 2, 1865. He left Richmond with all the papers of the Executive office on the special train containing the President, his staff, his cabinet (with the exception of the Secretary of War, General John C. Breckinridge) and many other government officials.

That train reached Danville, Virginia the late afternoon of the next day (April 3) and partially reorganized and opened the government offices. The business of the C.S.A. was conducted at the Benedict House on Wilson Street and at the Sutherlin Mansion on Main Street. The Confederate government remained there until the 10th of April when news of General R. E. Lee's surrender was received.

The guards left Danville with the treasure the 6th of April and went to Greensboro where they remained for a day and then continued on to Charlotte. As they approached Salisbury, North Carolina they spotted cavalry descending the hills in the vicinity "and we stopped to reconnoiter – for the times were troublous. It turned out to be some Confederate soldiers and they passed on. The guards reached Charlotte about the 8th."

W. H. Parker deposited the money in the mint as directed and left it in the custody of its proper officers. "I thought I was rid of it forever," he wrote. They remained in Charlotte several days. Upon attempting to telegraph the Secretary of the Navy, William Parker found the wires had been cut by General Stoneman who was then in possession of Salisbury, North Carolina with his command. It was supposed he would obtain information there concerning the treasure, and that he would soon make his appearance in Charlotte where there were no troops to oppose him. Lt. Parker was the senior naval officer present on duty in Charlotte and had to decide as to the necessary steps to preserve the treasure.

Parker decided to move the treasure further south to Georgia.

The last official act of President Davis was to name M. H. Clark Acting Treasurer. The following is Clark's final report:

I turned over $108,322.90 to the credit of Major E. C. White, Quartermaster, to pay troops marching through Georgia. He made this payment based upon the request of John C. Breckenridge, Sec. of War and "indorsed" by John H. Reagan, Acting Secretary of the Treasury.

Additional payments were made to the Quartermaster's department (Specie $5,000), to the officers and men of the President's guard ($1,454 in silver), to E. H. Burns for one month's pay ($18), to A. G. Cantley of the Post Office Department ($50 in specie), to Major J. Foster to pay troops under Breckenridge command ($4,000 in gold), to Assistant Paymaster, J. R. Wheless for the officers and midshipmen "pro rate according to rank" employed in guarding the treasure from Richmond to Abbeville ($1,500 in specie), to Lt. Bradford of the Marine Corps ($300 in silver . . . actually paid in gold), to General Braxton Bragg for transmission to the Trans-Mississippi Department ($2,000 in coin), to five commissioned officers and twenty-six men, belonging to Brigadier-General York's Louisiana Brigade ($806) in specie), to Capt. Joseph M. Brown for Quartermaster's Department ($520 in gold), to John C. Breckenridge for transmission to the Trans-Mississippi Department ($1,000 in specie) and to Major R. J. Moses (Twenty boxes supposed to be worth in coin from $35,000 to $40,000 in silver bullion but uncounted before verification of the amount).

He further reported "My last payment in Washington, Ga., was of eighty-six thousand dollars ($86,000) in gold coin and gold bullion, to a trusted officer of the navy, taking his receipt for its transmission out of the Confederacy, to be held for the Treasury Department."

The total value of specie and bullion disbursed in Washington, Georgia was $250,960.90. If the value of the treasure turned over to him in Greensboro, N.C. was $288,022.90, and he left $35,000 in gold sovereigns with President Davis and his Cabinet then he should still have had in his possession $2,062.00 when he departed Washington, Georgia at 11 p.m.

Clark suggested and Hon. John H. Reagan and Acting Secretary of the Treasury, concurred that the following payment be made:

Colonel John Taylor Wood .... $1,500 in gold
Colonel William Preston Johnston .... $1,500 in gold
Colonel F. R. Lubbock .... $1,500 in gold

He also gave each one $10 in silver for small uses, from a little executive fund he had established from an exchange of paper to silver in Danville.

Colonel C. E. Thorburn, a naval purchasing agent, took a receipt from each one for this specie which totaled $4,500 and leaving a negative balance of $2,448.

[Evidently, part of the $35,000 in gold left with the President and his Cabinet in Greensboro was subsequently returned to the Confederate treasure and used for these disbursements.]

Captain Clark left after making these disbursements. Secretary Reagan remained for a short time to transfer the treasure in his hands, except a few thousand dollars, and then joined Clark on the road.

This transfer of the treasure was made to Mr. Semple, a bonded officer of the Navy, and his assistant, Mr. Tidball, with instructions to transfer it abroad and deliver it to the commercial house which had acted as financial agent of the Confederate government as soon as it could be safely done. The best recollection was that the financial agent referred to was Fraser, Trenholm & Co., London, England.

In M. H. Clark's final report, why was there no mention of Mexican silver dollars? If, as Walter Philbrook reported, the bulk and weight of the Confederate treasure was in Mexican silver dollars and only one keg (4,000 of them) made it to Greensboro, what happened to the remaining $196,000?

Doesn't it make sense that the missing Mexican silver dollars must still be in Danville and no place else?

THE TREASURE IN RETROSPECT
A. Danville and No Place Else

Consider these indisputable facts:

The amount of specie leaving Richmond on the treasure train as reported by Walter Philbrook was between $500,000 and $600,000, the bulk and weight of which was in Mexican silver dollars.

The treasure train remained in Danville only two days. Even though it had been the intent of the Treasury Department to make exchanges in Danville, little business transpired.

When the treasure arrived in Greensboro, North Carolina, the last acting treasurer reported the amount of specie was $327,022.90.

Since the accounting of the Confederate treasure in Greensboro was only $327,022.90, very little had been exchanged in Danville, and only the one opened keg of Mexican silver dollars is ever mentioned again, it must be assumed that the kegs never left Danville.

If you add $200,000 in Mexican silver dollars (minus the $4,000 from the open keg that was distributed to Johnston's troops in Jamestown, North Carolina) the Greensboro accounting, the total treasure would have been $523,022.90.

A veritable fortune, forty-nine kegs of uncirculated Mexican silver dollars at $4,000 per keg for a total of $196,000 in face value must be concealed somewhere in the River City

Still not convinced? Perhaps *Five Questions Answered* will help you.

B. Five Questions Answered

For 131 years, a substantial portion of the Confederate Treasure has defied all attempts to be discovered. There are those who would scoff at the idea of buried Confederate treasure because of the following valid questions.

1. *Why didn't those who knew the location tell someone?*
   Honor, integrity and honesty would not permit them to even discuss the hiding place.
2. *Why did no one return to get the treasure after the War?*
   Their pardons precluded them from getting any monetary advantage from their connection to the Confederate Cause.
3. *With so much highway and building excavation over the past 131 years, why hasn't it been accidentally discovered?*
   Those who hid the treasure went so far as to foster false tales and alter records so that no one would ever discover the exact location.
4. *With so many people believing that the treasure is still extant, why hasn't a clever person found it?*
   In the final analysis I had to overlook honor, integrity, honesty, lies, deceit and tall tales to conclude that a portion of the Confederate treasure must remain in the Last Capital of the Confederacy.
   And finally . . .
5. *If the treasure were valued in the thousands of dollars and currently worth millions, why wasn't its location doggedly pursued?*
   In the past no one has really known what part of the treasure was missing and could, therefore, make no accounting of its worth. Perhaps now, with this new information, treasure hunters will be able to pinpoint its location.

The data and documentation found in this book targets the location of the *Confederate Treasure in Danville.*

EPILOGUE

Davis said that his whole heart and soul were still in the Cause. He would never consent to abandon a foot of Confederate soil, and if driven out of Virginia, he would be back.

Confederate Treasure in Danville brings us back to Virginia to visit a small portion of the Confederate government left to tantalize and challenge those who may have forgotten his resolve and prophecy.

Confederate Treasure in Danville begins in the Foreword with an example of how a sermon introduced my interest in the Confederate treasure and ends properly with an admonition by Trenholm to his son, another Frank, "Riches take to themselves wings and fly away, our wealth was great, but where is it?" He pointed out that "God alone can satisfy the soul. He alone can give us perpetual peace and contentment."

Francis Holmes Trenholm
(Courtesy of Frank Lyman)

BIBLIOGRAPHY

A Brief History Of The First Presbyterian Church, Danville, VA. 1826-1926.

Ainsworth, Fred C. and Kirkley, Joseph W. "The War Of The Rebellion: A Compilation Of The Offical Records Of The Union and ConfederateArmies. Washington, D.C.: Government Printing Office, 1900, p. 164.

Anderson, Frederick Jarrard. THE THIRD JUBILLE: A HISTORY OF THE FIRST BAPTIST CHURCH OF DANVILLE, VIRGINIA - 1834-1984. Danville, 1984.

Anderson, Joseph B. Manuscript in Alderman Library Collection, University of Virginia, Charlottesville.

"An Offical Guide of the Confederate Governments - From 1861 to 1865, Richmond". Ricketts Associates. Richmond, VA.

Baker, Nina Brown, JUAREZ, HERO OF MEXICO, Vanguard Press, 1942. New York.

Ball, Douglas, FINANCIAL FAILURE IN CONFEDERATE DEFEAT.

Ballard, M. B. LONG SHADOW: JEFFERSON DAVIS AND THE FINAL DAYS OF THE CONFEDERACY. 1986.

Birdsall, C. M. THE UNITED STATES BRANCH MINT AT CHARLOTTE, NORTH CAROLINA: ITS HISTORY AND COINAGE. 1988.

Birdsall, C. M. THE UNITED STATES BRANCH MINT AT DAHLONEGA, GEORGIA: ITS HISTORY AND COINAGE. Easley, South Carolina, 1986.

Births & Deaths, Circuit Court of Danville, VA. City of Danville, VA.

Brubaker, III, John H. THE LAST CAPITAL. Danville, 1979.

Cahill, Mary & Grant, Gary. VICTORIAN DANVILLE: 52 LANDMARKS, THEIR ARCHITECTURE & HISTORY. Danville, 1977.

Capers, Henry D. THE LIFE AND TIMES OF C G MEMMINGER. Richmond, 1893.

Catton, William & Bruce. TWO ROADS TO SUMTER. 1963; reprinted 1971.

Census Records, Virginia. 1850, 1860 & 1870 (In Danville Public Library).

"Chronology of the Old U. S. Mint." New Orleans: State Museum for the Old U. S. Mint.

Clark, James C., THE LAST TRAIN SOUTH

Clark, M. H. "The Last Days Of The Confederate Treasury And What Became Of Its Specie." Southern Historical Society Papers, IX, 542-556. 1881.

Confederate Veteran. (Published monthly from January 1893 through December, 1932, 40 Vols. Articles are valuable in part but not always accurate. "Confederate Naval Cadets," XII, 170-171, (April 1904). "The Last of the   C . S. Ordinance Department," XXXIV, 368-369, (October 1966) and XXXV, 15-16, (June 1927). "The Confederate Treasure Train," XXV, 257-259, (June 1917). "Last Of Confederate Treasury Department," XXXVII, 423-425, (Nov. 1929).

Coulter, E. Merton. THE CONFEDERATE STATES OF AMERICA: 1861-1865. Louisiana State University Press, Baton Rouge, LA. 1950.

Council Records, Danville, VA. 1833-1870. Engineering Department, City of Danville

Cunningham, H. H. DOCTORS IN GRAY. Binghamton, NY. 1958.

Daddysman, James W., 1936, the matamoros trade: confederate commerce, diplomacy, and intrigue. University of Delaware Press, 1984.

Dame, George Washington. HISTORICAL SKETCH OF ROMAN EAGLE LODGE NO. 122 A.F.& A.M., 1820-1895. Danville, 1939.

Danville Register. May 17, 1914 and April 13, 1919.

Davis, Burke. THE LONG SURRENDER. 1989.

Davis, Burke. TO APPOMATTOX: NINE APRIL DAYS, 1865. New York,   1959.

Davis, Jefferson. THE PAPERS OF JEFFERSON DAVIS, 6 VOLS. 1971-89.

Davis, Jefferson. THE RISE AND FALL OF THE CONFEDERATE GOVERNMENT. Volumes 1 & 2. New York, 1881.

Davis, W. C. JEFFERSON DAVIS. 1991.

Davis, William C. A GOVERNMENT OF OUR OWN, New York, 1994.

Deeds, Wills & Marriages, Circuit Court of Danville, VA. City of Danville, VA.

Donnelly, Ralph W. "The Charlotte Mint: 8c Balance.", in the Numismatist. Published in Colorado Springs, CO.

Dowdey, Clifford. EXPERIMENT IN REBELLION. New York, 1946.

Dufour, Charles L. THE NIGHT THE WAR WAS LOST. New York: Doubleday & Co., 1960.

Durkin, J. T. STEPHEN R. MALLORY: CONFEDERATE NAVY CHIEF. 1954.

Eaton, Clement. JEFFERSON DAVIS, THE SPHINX OF THE CONFEDERACY. New York, 1977.

Folk, Winston. "A Treasure Hunt In Reverse." United States Naval Institute Proceedings, LXIII, 380-387, March, 1937.

Fountain, Clara. DANVILLE: A PICTORIAL HISTORY. Virginia Beach, 1979.

Freeman, Douglas S. R E LEE. Vol. 4, New York, 1935.

Gibbs, William T. "No Blood Shed In Seizure Of Charlotte Mint: Fire, Civil War Disrupt Coinage At Branch Mint In NC." Coin World Magazine, Feb. 25, 1987.

Gilliam, Robert. "Reminisces Of A Former Confederate Treasury Clerk." 1952.

Hairston, Beatrice. A BRIEF HISTORY OF DANVILLE: 1728-1954. Danville, 1955.

Hagan, Jane Gray. STORY OF DANVILLE. Danville, 1950.

Hall, Raymond. CHURCH OF THE EPIPHANY, DANVILLE, VA, CENTENNIAL 1840-1940. Danville, 1940.

Hanna, A. J. FLIGHT INTO OBLIVION. Richmond, 1938.

Harrison, Mrs. Burton. RECOLLECTIONS, GRAVE AND GAY. New York 1912.

Harrison, Kathy G, eorge & Busey, John W. NOTHING BUT GLORY: PICKETT'S DIVISION AT GETTYSBURG. Gettysburg, 1987; reprinted 1993.

Head, Sylvia & Etheridge, Elizabeth. THE NEIGHBORHOOD MINT AT DAHLONEGA IN THE AGE OF JACKSON.

Headlight Magazine, 1896. Published in Danville, VA.

Henderson, Dr. Archibald, in Greensboro, NC Daily News, September 1, 1935.

Hobbs, Ralph 803-635-5219 Winnsboro, SC Public Library 803-635-4971 803- 635-9811 WMF ASHMORE

Hodder, Michael J., "Technological Innovation At The New Orleans Mint.", in the Numismatist, April, 1991.

Hoke, Tom, "How The Mint Was Robbed.", in the Numismatist, September, 1994, Published in Colorado Springo, CO.

Hudgeons, Marc. OFFICIAL 1994 BLACKBOOK, PRICE GUIDE OF UNITED STATES COINS, New York, 1994.

Jacob Davis Notebook, 1855-1875. Danville, VA.
    Press, 1942.

Krause, Chester and Mischler, Clifford — Bruce, II, Colin, Editor. *1944 StandardCatalogue of World Coins.* 21st. Edition. Krause Publications. Iola, Wisconsin.

Lancaster, Robert Alexander, 1829-1902 papers, 1855-1890. Correspondence concerning the Treasury Department of the Confederate States of America.

Land Books, Circuit Court of Danville, VA. City of Danville, VA.

McElroy, Roberts. JEFFERSON DAVIS: THE UNREAL AND THE REAL, 2 VOLS. 1937; reprinted 1969.

Mack, Mary MacKenzie. HISTORY OF THE OLD GROVE STREET CEMETERY. Danville, 1939.

Mallory, Stephen R. Diary in Southern Historical Collection. Louis R. Wilson Library, University of North Carolina, Chapel Hill.

Maps, City of Danville, Virginia. 1816, 1847 (Annex), 1854, 1867, 1870.   Engineering Department, City of Danville.

Marriages, Deeds & Wills. Circuit Court Records, City of Danville.

Meade, Robert D. JUDAH P. BENJAMIN: CONFEDERATE STATESMAN. New York, 1943.

MEMORIALS OF THE LIFE, PUBLIC SERVICES AND CHARACTER OF WILLIAM T. SUTHERLIN. Danville, 1894.

Nepveux, Ethel Trenholm Seabrook, GEORGE ALFRED TRENHOLM: THE COMPANY THAT WENT TO WAR 1861-1865., Charleston, SC, 1973.

New York Times, Henry J. Raymond, Editor. April 12, May 1 and 28, and June 1, 1865 and January 6, 1882, accounts of the movements of the Confederate treasure train by Walter Philbrook, Chief Teller of the Confederate Treasury Department and others.

Nutt, William D., 1805 The Smith Family papers, 1796-1867. Letters written to William D. Nutt, Washington, DC.

Parker, William H., RECOLLECTIONS OF A NAVAL OFFICER. BY W. H. PARKER, New York, 1883.

Patrick, Robert. JEFFERSON DAVIS AND HIS CABINET. 1944; reprinted 1976.

Pollock, Edward. ILLUSTRATED SKETCH BOOK OF DANVILLE, VIRGINIA. Danville, 1885.

Richmond, Virginia, Times, P. H. Aylett, Editor. "The Confederate Treasure," X, 137-141. (March, 1882).

Ricketts, Danny. CHARTS, MAPS & POSTERS. Danville.

Robertson, James I., Jr. Centennial address at Danville, Apr. 3, 1965, published in the Danville Register April 4, 1965.

Robertson, James I., Jr. HOUSES OF HORROR: DANVILLE'S CIVIL WAR PRISONS. Virginia Magazine of History and Biography, 69. July, 1961.

Roder, Ralph. JUAREZ AND HIS MEXICO, The Viking Press, 1947. New York.

Roe, Alfred S. "In A Rebel Prison or Experiences In Danville, VA". Reprinted in R. D. Ricketts. 1984, Danville, VA.

Rolle, Andrew F. THE LOST CAUSE: THE CONFEDERATE EXODUS TO MEXICO. University of Oklahoma Press, 1965. Norman, Oklahoma.

Rosen, Robert N. A SHORT HISTORY OF CHARLESTON. Peninsula Press,Charleston, 1982.

Rosen, Robert N. CONFEDERATE CHARLESTON. University of South Carolina Press, Columbia, SC, 1994

Rowland, Dunbar, ed. JEFFERSON DAVIS: CONSTITUTIONALIST, HIS LETTERS, PAPERS, AND SPEECHES. Vol. 6, Jackson, Miss. 1923.

Scholes, Walter B. MEXICAN POLITICS DURING THE JUAREZ REGIME. The University of Missouri Studies, 1957. Columbia, Missouri

Semmes, Raphael. MEMOIRS OF SERVICE AFLOAT DURING THE WAR BETWEEN THE STATES. Baltimore, 1869.

Smith, Ernest. THE HISTORY OF THE CONFEDERATE TREASURY. 1901.

Southern History Association Publications "History of the Confederate Treasury," V, 1-34, 95-150, 188-227, (January, March and May, 1901).

Spence, E. Lee. TREASURES OF THE CONFEDERATE COAST: THE "REAL RHETT BUTLER" & OTHER REVELATIONS. Miami/Charleston, Narwhal Press, 1995.

Strode, Hudson, ed. JEFFERSON DAVIS: PRIVATE LETTERS. New York, 1966.

Strode, Hudson, ed. JEFFERSON DAVIS: TRAGIC HERO. New York, 1964.

Tax Books, Circuit Court of Danville, VA. City of Danville, VA.

Thian, Raphael P. REGISTER OF THE CONFEDERATE DEBT. Boston, 1972.

Thompson, William Young. ROBERT TOOMBS OF GEORGIA. 1966.

Todd, Richard C. CONFEDERATE FINANCE. ATHENS, ga. 1954.

Vandiver, Frank E. JEFFERSON DAVIS AND THE CONFEDERATE STATE. 1964.

VA/NC Piedmont Genealogical Society. GREEN HILL CEMETERY, DANVILLE, VIRGINIA. (1833-1986) VOLS I & II. Danville, 1988.

Vertical Files, Danville Public Library

Wesley, Charles, H. THE COLLAPSE OF THE CONFEDERACY. Washington,   1937.

Wharton, H. M.: WAR SONGS & POEMS OF THE CONFEDERACY, by H.   M. WHARTON. 1904, N.P.

Willingham, Robert M., Jr. NO JUBILEE: THE STORY OF CONFEDERATE WILKES. Washington, Georgia, 1976.

Wise, John S. THE END OF AN ERA. Boston, 1899.

Withers, Robert E. AUTOBIOGRAPHY OF AN OCTOGENARIAN. Roanoke, 1907.

Woodworth, S. E. JEFFERSON DAVIS AND HIS GENERALS. 1990.

Yeoman, R. S. A GUIDEBOOK OF UNITED STATES COINS. 47th EDITION. Racine, Wisconsin, 1994.

Young, Cassye A. LAST CAPITAL OF THE CONFEDERACY, DANVILLE, VIRGINIA. Danville, after 1954.